*Teach Like a Disciple*

# Teach Like a Disciple

Exploring Jesus' Instructive Relationships
from an Educational Perspective

Jillian Nerhus Lederhouse

WIPF & STOCK · Eugene, Oregon

TEACH LIKE A DISCIPLE
Exploring Jesus' Instructive Relationships from an Educational Perspective

Copyright © 2016 Jillian Nerhus Lederhouse. All rights reserved. Except for brief quotations in critical publications or reviews, no part of this book may be reproduced in any manner without prior written permission from the publisher. Write: Permissions, Wipf and Stock Publishers, 199 W. 8th Ave., Suite 3, Eugene, OR 97401.

Wipf & Stock
An Imprint of Wipf and Stock Publishers
199 W. 8th Ave., Suite 3
Eugene, OR 97401

www.wipfandstock.com

PAPERBACK ISBN: 978-1-4982-8979-5
HARDCOVER ISBN: 978-1-4982-8981-8
EBOOK ISBN: 978-1-4982-8980-1

Manufactured in the U.S.A.                                      10/31/16

Scriptures taken from the Holy Bible, New International Version®, NIV®. Copyright © 1973, 1978, 1984, 2011 by Biblica, Inc.™ Used by permission of Zondervan. All rights reserved worldwide. www.zondervan.com The "NIV" and "New International Version" are trademarks registered in the United States Patent and Trademark Office by Biblica, Inc.™

*To
Julia, Nancy, and Sally,
who have taught me by their examples
how to teach like a disciple*

# Contents

1. Teach Like a Disciple | 1
2. The Relational Jesus and the Heartbroken Student | 10
3. The Demanding Jesus and the Student Who Craved Success | 19
4. The Holistic Jesus and the Student Who Needed Healing | 31
5. The Multicultural Jesus and the Student Who Needed Acceptance | 42
6. The Challenging Jesus and the Gifted Student | 54
7. The Patient Jesus and the Student Who Craved Attention | 65
8. The Perceptive Jesus and the Quiet Student | 79
9. The Provocative Jesus and the Judgmental Student | 91
10. The Purposeful Jesus and the Students Who Wanted Him to Please Them | 105
11. The Transforming Jesus and the Student No One Believed in | 118
12. Parting Words | 131

*Bibliography* | 137

# 1

# Teach Like a Disciple

As an adult Christian, I have always been intrigued by the Apostle John's words at the conclusion of his Gospel:

> Jesus performed many other signs in the presence of his disciples, which are not recorded in this book. But these are written that you may believe that Jesus is the Messiah, the Son of God, and that by believing you might have life through his name. (John 20:30–31)

> This is the disciple who testifies to these things and who wrote them down. We know that his testimony is true. Jesus did many other things as well. If every one of them were written down, I suppose that even the whole world would not have room for the books that would be written. (John 21:24–25)

Because of these references, I have often wondered what other signs or miracles Jesus performed and what impact he had on the individuals who witnessed these amazing acts. Three years of a teaching ministry had to produce a large number of conversations and supernatural events, no doubt requiring the four authors of the Gospels to leave many of these interactions out of their written accounts. This insight, in turn, has led me to wonder what specific criteria the Holy Spirit and gospel writers used for determining which signs and encounters would lead to a saving knowledge of Jesus Christ and which ones would not be instrumental to this process. These criteria for inclusion would create an amazing rubric, wouldn't they? I can picture Luke looking at his outlined list and deciding to include the account of the crippled woman healed on the Sabbath but determining that the healing of another individual should not "make the cut." I look forward someday in heaven to learning this rationale and to hearing all these other individuals tell their perhaps less instrumental but still significant, life-changing stories.

These two questions have led me to a conclusion. Since these Spirit-led authors followed a careful selection process for relating Jesus' impact on our world, those encounters that were included must be critically important for us to study. They deserve our repeated attention even after our journey to conversion. Jesus himself did not come to simply write down the plan of salvation for us; rather, his ministry focused on teaching others, healing others, and ultimately saving others. His was always a relational ministry. The authors of the gospels recorded his engaging interactions with those he sought out and those who searched for him. In effect, Matthew, Mark, Luke, and John's task was, in large part, to record the lesson plans of the Master Teacher. Although Jesus' objectives may not have been aligned to state or national standards, these exemplary lessons provided a powerful means for understanding that God loved humankind to such a degree that he sacrificed his only Son for our redemption.

Although much has been written about teaching from a biblical, Christ-centered perspective,[1] few of these books have started from Christ's relationships with specific individuals. It is my hope that through these instructive relationships, we can be teachers who follow Jesus' example in engaging our students and communicating how we value *them* along with the wonders and realities of the world we inhabit. My goal in studying Jesus' content and pedagogy within these stories is that we will learn to teach with the same mind-set he taught. As his followers, we will gain a better understanding of how to teach like a follower of Christ—how to teach like a disciple.

---

1. See Graham, *Teaching Redemptively*; Von Brummelen, *Walking with God*; and Wolterstorff, *Educating for Life*.

## Why should teachers study these relationships?

The first reason we should study Jesus' relationships is that God himself is relational, as defined most succinctly in 1 John 4:8: "Whoever does not love does not know God, because God is love." One cannot love without being relational, because genuine love must be directed toward others. The overarching theme of Scripture is the redemptive story of a God who loved his creation even after it rejected him. This love was so great that he rescued it through the sacrifice of his own Son, Jesus. Throughout the Old Testament, God revealed this plan of rescue through covenants with Adam, Noah, Abraham, Moses, and David.[2] These covenants, which reflected God's unfailing love, were his promises to those who were faithful in their relationship to him.

In the New Testament, we see a loving relationship between the Father and the Son expressed in the prayer Jesus offered at Gethsemane. Within this prayer, we see both their love for each other and the love Jesus has for his followers, as indicated by his desire that they experience the same type of relationship he had with his Father. "I have made you known to them and will continue to make you known in order that the love you have for me may be in them and that I myself may be in them" (John 17:26). This prayer, offered just minutes before his arrest, trial, and crucifixion, demonstrates the depth of his love for us and his commitment to God's rescue plan. This commitment resulted in a new covenant through which Christ's sacrifice provided a ransom for our sin, enabling us to receive the promise of a great inheritance (Heb 9:15). The Father's love for us is also communicated in Paul's Letter to the Romans. He writes, "He who did not spare his own Son but gave him up for us all, how will he not also, along with him, graciously give us all things?" (Rom 8:32).

The relational aspects of the Holy Spirit were promised by Jesus when he assured the apostles that they would not be alone after he returned to his Father:

---

2. Richter, *Epic of Eden*, 69–91.

> I will ask the Father, and he will give you another advocate to help you and be with you forever—the Spirit of truth. The world cannot accept him, because it neither sees him nor knows him. But you know him, for he lives with you and will be in you. (John 14:16–17)

We are so privileged to be loved by such a relational God.

The second reason for this type of study is that good teaching is relational. Charlotte Danielson, creator of the "Framework for Teaching," a structure that is used for teacher evaluation in most states, devotes an entire domain to the teacher-student relationship and the guidance he or she provides for student-to-student relationships. Both of these components are critical to forming a positive classroom environment for learning. She states, "Teaching depends, fundamentally, on the quality of relationships among individuals."[3]

Parker Palmer also emphasizes the importance of the relationship between student, teacher, and content in *The Courage to Teach*:

> Good teachers possess a capacity for connectedness. They are able to weave a complex web of connections among themselves, their subjects and their students so that students can learn to weave a world for themselves...The connections made by good teachers are held not in their methods but in their hearts.[4]

Professional educators rely on their ability to connect to learners and connect those learners with content, but teachers also need the ability to read people as well as the textbooks that supplement their instruction. Although they use this skill to determine whether students understand a new concept, this type of social perception extends beyond academics. When students or parents walk into a classroom, teachers need to perceive their emotional states by reading nonverbal cues. If visitors show signs of being upset, teachers need to be able to quickly determine whether they

---

3. Danielson, *Enhancing Professional Practice*, 64.
4. Palmer, *Courage to Teach*, 11.

are angry, heartbroken, resigned to an outcome, or ready to protest. Teachers also need to determine whether the conflict is due to something they have done or due to a school policy, or if it is personal in nature. The ability to connect well with a diverse group of learners, parents, and colleagues is a rather sophisticated but essential interpersonal demand of the profession.

The third reason for studying the relationships of Jesus comes out of a need for justice. Teaching is a complex profession, but one of its key components is to make a rich and rigorous curriculum accessible to every learner. This would not be challenging if every learner had the same background experiences, economic resources, interests, and primary language. But this has not been the case. The history of American public education can be characterized as a struggle for educational equity. It chronicles the broadening of learning opportunities to include women, students of color, particularly students who are non-native English speakers, as well as those students who require special education services in order to achieve their academic potential.[5] But school achievement today is still determined largely by economic factors. What you learn and how you think are often dependent upon the wealth of your family and school community. Yet research has indicated that teachers committed to implementing culturally responsive pedagogy can make a significant difference. Eric Jensen states, "The relationships that teachers build with students form the single strongest access to student goals, socialization, motivation and academic performance."[6]

For educators who are committed to serving Christ, teaching and advocating for educational justice are not optional. They are required elements of being individually and corporately obedient to him. Timothy Keller writes:

> The justness of a society, according to the Bible, is evaluated by how it treats these groups [widows, the fatherless, immigrants, the poor]. Any neglect shown ... is not

---

5. See Banks and Banks, *Multicultural Education*; Gutek, *Historical and Philosophical Foundations*; and Ladson-Billings, *Dreamkeepers*.

6. Jensen, *Teaching with Poverty in Mind*, 20.

called merely a lack of mercy or charity, but a violation of justice, of *mishpat*. God loves and defends those with the least economic and social power, and so should we. That is what it means to "do justice."[7]

Jesus' response to the individual, despite the dictates of unjust cultural norms and poverty, consistently communicated respect, inclusiveness, and empathy for his diverse students. He has much to teach us about "loving our neighbor" within an educational context.

## What does this study involve?

Each of the subsequent chapters focuses on an interaction between Jesus and, most often, one other individual. I refer to these individuals as students not only because the term fits with our profession and purposes but chiefly because these interactions provided a one-on-one opportunity for these individuals to learn something significant from the Master Teacher. As in our own practice, some students learned their lessons well; others failed. And for some, we are uncertain if or when they ever achieved Jesus' objective for them. Also similar to our own practice, this collection of individuals comprised a highly diverse group of students with specific needs: wealthy and poor, women and men, unschooled and well-educated, the boisterous and the nearly silent, those Jesus knew well and those who were strangers to him, those of his own faith and cultural tradition and those well outside it, and those in high standing as well as those who were powerless. These individuals are still found in our classrooms today.

Each chapter follows the same framework of answering five questions: What do we know about this student? What do we know about Jesus from this interaction? What can we learn from this student? What can we learn from Jesus in this interaction? What can we, as educators, learn from this interaction?

---

7. Keller, *Generous Justice*, 5.

The first question explores the identity of the student from the context of the passage and our knowledge of his or her culture at the time of the writing. Just as our practice must take into account the needs and priorities of our students, Jesus' own instruction drew upon the background of his learner. The second question focuses on what we know about Jesus from the context of this interaction, his approach to instruction, and the manner in which he related to his learner. The third question helps us understand what the student has to teach us. Each one demonstrated incredible competencies as well as specific needs, and we need to appreciate both their strengths and weaknesses as Jesus did. The fourth guiding question examines what we can learn from Jesus through this passage, what truth he communicated, and the way he related to his student throughout his lesson, including his or her response. And finally, the last question is specific to us as teachers. It focuses on what we can apply, as either beginning or experienced educators, from Jesus' specific encounter with this student. It examines the characteristics Jesus demonstrated, so that we can emulate them in our professional practice.

I would recommend that you read the identified biblical passage given at the start of the chapter before reading my text. Although all of the accounts may be quite familiar to you, I ask you to read them again through the lens of a teacher. Focus on what remains consistent in Jesus' teaching across these ten interactions and what changes in his approach from student to student.

The challenge in writing this book has been to take a global truth offered in Jesus' curriculum or pedagogy and see its practical application to our profession without trivializing Jesus' message. While I want us to be able to see Jesus in the role of teacher, I do not want to communicate anything less than the Holy Spirit intended us to learn from these passages. When my oldest daughter was four years of age, I would typically ask her what she had learned in her morning Sunday school lesson. I was often amused by her lesson's developmentally appropriate but somewhat tangential objective. For example, one of her responses to my question was, "We learned a boy shared his lunch with Jesus." Although this learning goal about sharing was fitting for a child her age, it completely overlooked the astounding miracle of feeding 5,000 people from the small boy's lunch.

I do not want to commit this same type of omission here. I don't want us to neglect the miracle for the sake of a teaching principle. The richness of Scripture enables us to return to it time after time and find new insights in the text. However, I do not want to neglect Scripture's powerful and eternal purposes for the sake of finding isolated connections to teaching. I am not aiming to substitute one meaning for another, nor am I attempting to turn our Bible into a textbook for a methods course. My intent is not to sideline its key themes but rather to illustrate how Jesus communicated these eternal truths through a carefully chosen instructional approach—one that brought out the truth in a way that was most accessible to his specific student.

I also do not want to imply that the only thing we need to do in order to teach effectively is to read our Bible. This is not true for teaching any more than it would be to read Scripture to learn how to farm. Our Bibles are not a substitute for a carefully sequenced set of courses and mentored clinical experiences to learn the art and science of teaching.

On the other hand, too often we compartmentalize our spiritual identity by separating it from our professional practice, especially if we teach in a public school context. Dallas Willard in *The Divine Conspiracy* writes, "If I am Jesus' disciple that means *I am with him to learn from him how to be like him*."[8] We know that Jesus was a teacher who has much to offer us for salvation and godly living, but we may not think to look at his practice for valuable elements of good teaching.

Whether you are a student planning to teach or an experienced professional educator, I hope that the insights offered in this book will be valuable to you. I have often said that the Christian life has a lot in common with a ninth-grade health course. Both domains deal with information that is easy to learn but so difficult to put into practice. We all know that we need to eat less fat, avoid

---

8. Willard, *Divine Conspiracy*, 303.

stress and high-risk behaviors, and exercise more, but knowing this information is not enough to maintain a healthy lifestyle. We need to act on this knowledge on a consistent basis, which requires discipline. Looking at any random group of people will attest to how difficult it is to put good habits into practice. In the same way, we all know we need to love our neighbor, obey God's commands, and practice the spiritual disciplines. We often start out well but soon struggle to maintain a meaningful devotional life or to hold our tongue when adversity confronts us.

Similarly, we all know to care for our students, differentiate their instruction, and be patient with their progress. But as teachers, we have all had days when we fell short of our professional aspirations. We have lost our temper with a colleague, failed to find the right accommodation for a student because we gave up too quickly, or skimmed over a homework assignment that needed more of our careful evaluation. Knowing what to do is very different from implementing it. In all three domains—health, the Christian life, and the Christian teacher's professional life—we strive daily to do better than the day before.

I ultimately hope and trust that as a result of this study, you will think of Christ's example when relating to your heartbroken, quiet, or attention-demanding student. You will think of Jesus' approach when challenging your gifted student. And most of all, you will emulate the Master Teacher when seeking to establish a relationship with the student everyone else has given up on. You will teach like his disciple.

2

# The Relational Jesus and the Heartbroken Student

## *John 20:1–18*

I BELIEVE JESUS' INTERACTION with Mary Magdalene, as recorded in John 20:1–18, is one of the most remarkable accounts in Scripture and reveals more to us about Jesus' nature than any other passage. Because of this, it is critically important for us as teachers to pay attention to the lessons it holds for us. It tells us how to balance what is to be learned with who it is that must learn it.

### What do we know about Mary Magdalene?

We know from the account in Luke 8:1–2 that Mary Magdalene had been healed by Jesus of seven demons. Her hometown of Magdala was located on the Galilee coast, a mile's distance from Jerusalem. We also learn from this passage that she was healed with two other women, Joanna and Susanna, who similarly became disciples of Jesus and supported him from their own means. Mary Magdalene befriended these women along with Mary, the mother of James. Scripture most often mentions Mary Magdalene in the company of several other women, so we can assume that she was one who enjoyed being with other followers of Jesus.

I am amazed at the particular attention the Holy Spirit places on individuals' names throughout Scripture. Think how much easier it would be for us to read Scripture without having to stumble over particular names of people and their hometowns—names and places that are often unfamiliar to our cultures today. Think of how much easier it would have been for Moses to just record that twelve groups of Hebrews went into the desert outside Egypt, but he meticulously lists each tribe and its leader. In Exod 31:1-5, we read about the individual men God called to build the tabernacle. Moses could have left their names out as well and simplified his account. Similarly, in the gospels we read about a man Jesus met in a tree, a man whose daughter was healed, and the name of the individual whose house Jesus visited. In both the Old and New Testaments, great attention is placed on individuals' identities by naming them. I believe this was done for two purposes.

First, it provides evidence that these events really happened. When a crime or other important event occurs today, one of the first steps in an investigation is to get the names and addresses of all eyewitnesses to the event. This brings credibility to the narrative. I believe the inclusion of names was important to the authors of Scripture as well. It makes their message more compelling to gather the evidence from similarly identified individuals.

Second and more importantly, it reveals that the individual is important to God. He knew their names; he knew them. After Abraham and Sarah's servant, Hagar, fled her mistress, she met the angel of the Lord in the desert. When he addressed her by name and offered her hope, she cried out, "You are the God who sees me" (Gen 16:13).

In John 10, Jesus likens himself to the good shepherd, stating that he knows his sheep and calls them each by name (John 10:14). Just as with the Israelites, we are not one in a crowd of nameless followers. We are recognized for our unique personalities; we are known by God.

Mary Magdalene knew Jesus well and because of her relationship to him became totally committed to him and his mission, even when circumstances became difficult. She remained with Jesus when many others had deserted him. All four gospels record that she was with him at the cross (Matt 27:61, Mark 15:40, Luke 23:49, John 19:25). We also learn from the Matthew and Luke accounts that Mary Magdalene was one of several women who helped to bury Jesus after his crucifixion (Matt 27:61, Luke 23:55–56), and all four gospels record that she was the first person to witness Christ's physical resurrection (Matt 28:1, Mark 16:1, Luke 24:1, John 20:1). She was no fair-weather fan of Jesus; rather, she was loyal to him at all costs. She was a woman of remarkable courage.

## What do we know about Jesus from this interaction?

Jesus took time to teach Mary along with his other disciples. This is an important issue where we again see that Jesus is quite unconventional. It was not typical for women to receive religious instruction. Unlike Hebrew boys at that time, girls were not students in the synagogue and therefore did not receive formal instruction in matters of faith or theology. But you never hear Jesus telling women that they are not capable of understanding his teaching. To the contrary, in Luke 10 Jesus tells Martha, who complained about her sister Mary's failure to help in the kitchen, that her sibling had chosen a better role—that of student—over hostess (Luke 10:41–42). Because Jesus did not select his students on the basis of gender, Mary Magdalene was welcomed into his classroom.

Looking at the passage of John 20:1-18, we learn some valuable insights from a thoughtful writer, the Apostle John. First, we learn that Mary and her two friends—Joanna and Mary, the mother of James—were the first to go to the tomb, even before John and Peter. When they saw that the stone had been moved, Mary Magdalene was frantic, assuming someone had stolen the body of Jesus. She sought help from Peter and John by running back to alert them. When the disciples ran to the tomb, they too found it empty, but they went back home. Apparently, Mary was not going to get their help in locating Jesus' body.

Mary alone stayed behind, standing outside the tomb weeping. Then she looked into the burial place and found two angels sitting on the very site that two days ago had held Jesus' body. They asked her why she was crying.

I often wished I could have heard how they asked her this question. Were they trying to offer sympathy, or were they genuinely puzzled since they already knew that Jesus was alive, having fulfilled his own prophecy? I think their inflection would have given us this insight.

Mary responded in a telling manner. She replied, "They have taken *my* Lord away, and I don't know where they have put him" (John 20:13). Unlike Peter during Jesus' trial, Mary identified with him. She wanted to claim his body; she felt responsible for him.

Through her tears, she noticed another man standing nearby. He asked her the same question the angels had asked, then asked her who it was that she was looking for. I would imagine he asked that second question with a smile. But Mary was weeping so uncontrollably that she could not identify the man by his voice or appearance and therefore assumed that he was a groundskeeper. She answered him, "Sir, if you have carried him away, tell me where you have put him, and I will get him" (John 20:15). Even single-handedly, she was committed to preserving Jesus' dignity.

The Lord then called her by name, "Mary." I think this has to be the most tender moment in all of Scripture. No gardener or groundskeeper would have known her name. It could be no one else except Jesus. She turned to him and, I am sure, had her second good cry of the morning, but now she was shedding tears of incredible happiness.

Although this passage contains a compassionate conversation, it is more than just a sweet story. This is an important event. Jesus had accomplished the most significant act in all of human history. He had just redeemed the human race from death and condemnation. He had triumphed over Satan and all the powers of darkness. Heaven had conquered hell. The Son had restored humankind's relationship with the Father, which had been broken since the garden of Eden. He had completed everything the Father had asked of him. His work was finished.

All of heaven was waiting to celebrate this great triumph. I can picture the angel chorus holding their pitch and the musicians watching for the downbeat from their conductor's baton. The celestial balloons were ready to be released at the moment the Guest of Honor arrived. Everything was perfectly in order for the glorious homecoming of the victorious Son.

Except for one thing.

There was a heartbroken woman crying in another garden—a cemetery, actually. Jesus had something he needed to do before the celestial celebration could begin. He needed to reassure a follower that everything was all right. For the first time since Eden, things were truly right again. So while all of heaven waited, he went to her and comforted her.

## What can we learn from Mary Magdalene?

We first learn that Mary kept her commitments. She understood that following Jesus was difficult, but she remained loyal to him in her friendship and trust. Even when she believed that the cause was lost, she remained committed to doing all she could for him. Even when she did not understand the circumstances, she did not abandon him. We can learn so much from her example of loyalty.

Second, Mary was courageous. After the crucifixion, Peter, John, and her other friends had gone back home. Even the guards who had been placed outside the tomb had deserted their posts when the supernatural event of the resurrection took place. But Mary was there with her two friends. Luke's account of the resurrection tells us that the three women initially saw two men inside the tomb in clothes that "gleamed like lightning" (Luke 24:4), but the women didn't run from them. When the angels addressed the women, these celestial beings referenced how Jesus had foretold his death when he was with the three in Galilee. These Galilean women were now in Jerusalem. How did these men know this information about them? It had to be unnerving, but Mary Magdalene remained despite her fear.

Third, Mary was a person of action. She didn't stay home and worry about things. She didn't stay home, period. Her home was in Galilee, but she followed her healer and teacher to learn everything she could from him. When her Savior was taken into custody, tried, and sentenced, she didn't abandon him. She supported him, standing by him in his darkest hour. She helped prepare his body for burial in the short time allotted before the Sabbath. When she went to complete that sad task on Sunday, she worked to find his body when it was no longer in the tomb. She was no passive, swooning female. She was decisive and determined to do the right thing, even when no one else was supporting her.

I have often wondered what forged these qualities in Mary Magdalene. Why was she so devoted when people even closer to Jesus were not? I cannot claim to know for certain, but I think it was because she recognized how Jesus had transformed her life. She remembered what her life was like before she had met Jesus and was healed, and she could clearly see the difference he had brought to her existence. She was a walking picture of the power of God, and she realized that she owed Christ everything.

We are also totally transformed because of Christ's work in our lives, but perhaps we may not have experienced the contrasts that Mary Magdalene so clearly observed. She is a wonderful reminder of Christ's ability to bring us from the brink of despair to a place of hope and joy, both in Galilee when Jesus healed her and outside the tomb in Jerusalem when he called her by name.

## What can we learn from Jesus in this interaction?

Just as Jesus mattered to Mary, Mary mattered to Jesus. I think this is a remarkable truth. Jesus could have so easily perceived that Mary's heartbreak was insignificant in light of his global mission, but he chose to take the time to relieve her burden. Despite redeeming all of humanity, Jesus needed to mend the hurt of one individual. You cannot be more personal than this. If you have ever questioned whether God was invested in your relationship with him, all doubt is dispelled by this account. If you have ever wondered whether God understands your personal heartbreak, there is much comfort is this account. Mary mattered to Jesus. We matter to Jesus, corporately and individually. You matter to Jesus.

Women mattered to Jesus. He not only allowed and encouraged women to learn from him and to become his followers, he chose one woman to bring the best and most important message ever told. Mary Magdalene was commissioned by Christ to tell the apostles, "I have seen the Lord!" (John 20:18).

This account also defines an appropriate relationship between Mary and Jesus. Although some works of fiction have caused several to question whether there was anything romantic or improper between Mary and Jesus, this account helps us understand their friendship. When Mary recognized him as Jesus rather than the gardener, she called him "Rabboni," which is to say, "Teacher." This is a formal term of respect, not of mutuality or endearment. There was also no embrace. In fact, Jesus tells her not to hold on to him because he needed to return to the Father. Theirs was a solid relationship between teacher and student.

Jesus tells her to inform his disciples of his destination. His words are significant. He says to tell them, "I am returning to my Father and your Father, to my God and your God." Because of his death and resurrection, Jesus' redemptive act enabled his Father God to be ours as well. Our relationship to God was changed by this rescue. We were once again the children of God. This is the very privileged message he gave to Mary Magdalene. She must have experienced the most extreme emotional swing of her life that day, going from despondency to incredible elation. And being the person of action that she was, Christ gave her the task of being the first to proclaim the gospel message of complete redemption.

## What can we, as educators, learn from this interaction?

How do we take the lessons from this powerful account into our classrooms? This passage relates the importance of developing a strong but appropriate rapport with our students. Even though Mary would soon have learned of his resurrection without Jesus personally appearing to her, he found it important to spend this time with her in order to end her distress. He put her needs ahead of his own agenda. While all of heaven waited, he cared for her.

## The Relational Jesus and the Heartbroken Student

Frequently in my career, I have needed to meet with a student, adjust aspects of a course requirement, extend grace on a deadline, or just create the space for a student to release an emotional burden he or she was carrying. Sometimes it was directly related to my course, and other times it was completely separate from academic stress. Students need and deserve to know they matter to us as people as well as learners. Jesus' interaction with Mary Magdalene reminds us to view each student as a complete individual, not just the "one who struggles with English vocabulary in our fourth period class."

From this account, I have learned that there is no appointment, no phone call, and no issue that is more important to resolve than meeting with a student who is troubled. If Jesus could delay his triumphant return to heaven for a heartbroken woman, I can delay my agenda for a student who needs me. I need to develop the ability to "read" my students and provide a space for them to seek my help. This is true in my current role as an education professor, but it was equally true when I taught kindergarten and other grades. All of my students, no matter what their age, need a classroom or office that provides safety. They also need an adult who can provide empathy, advice, or advocacy as the situation requires.

From this story, we learn too that Jesus related to Mary appropriately. Their interaction reflected a strong relationship between a teacher and pupil. Jesus established boundaries to develop the relationship in a manner that benefitted his student most. I find it helpful to realize that Jesus was not "on call" twenty-four-seven for his apostles, followers, or strangers. Surely, he could have spent all his time healing and preaching, but he did not do this. He built in significant time for rest and communication with his Father. While he was aware of needs, he was not need-driven.

As educators, we need to care for our students, but we also need to safeguard space within our schedules for self-care—rest, reflection, and restoration—in order to care for our students appropriately and to serve them well. This is especially challenging for teachers in their first year of practice when planning and grading outside of the school day seem to take up more time than actually instructing students. But Jesus is our model even in seeking time away from our professional responsibilities.

Many education scholars agree that caring is an essential quality of effective teaching. Philosopher Nel Noddings emphasizes the importance of caring for students and teaching students to care for themselves, for others, and the environment.[1] Sonia Nieto writes of the importance of continuing to stand in solidarity with one's students and offering them empathy despite today's pressures to focus merely on student achievement.[2] Steele and Cohn-Vargas stress the importance of teachers creating an environment where all students are accepted and encouraged.[3]

Many times, it is our smallest action rather than our help in a major crisis that students remember best. It may be calling them at home when they have missed class or done well on an assignment. Perhaps it is affirming them for being thoughtful toward another student when they didn't think we had noticed. But it always requires taking time to show we value them, just as Christ took time for Mary Magdalene. To teach like a disciple of Jesus, we need to communicate our care for students in a sensitive and appropriate manner.

---

1. See Noddings, *Caring: A Relational Approach*.
2. See Nieto, "Public Schools," 9–20.
3. See Steele and Cohn-Vargas, *Identity Safe Classrooms*.

3

# The Demanding Jesus and the Student Who Craved Success

## Mark 10:17–27

SINCE JESUS' ENCOUNTER WITH the rich young ruler is recorded in all three Synoptic Gospels (Matt 19:16–26, Mark 10:17–27, Luke 18:18–23), it must have made a significant impact on each of those authors. This may be due to Jesus' surprising request of this student and their conversation's unexpected conclusion. If we, as teachers, were to design a profile of our ideal student, I would imagine that it would match many of this young man's characteristics. We would all probably want this accomplished and motivated student to be in our own classrooms. However, the end of this encounter shows a highly successful student failing to grasp life's most important lesson. Like the reaction of the disciples, we are amazed that Jesus would require so much from his learner.

### What do we know about the rich young ruler?

As would likely be true in today's culture, this young man appears to be more famous for being rich than for being obedient to the law. From his conversation with Jesus, we learn that he had not only acquired or managed his wealth, he had also met the requirements of the law as he agreed to every command Jesus enumerated and assured him that he had obeyed them all since childhood. He was a religious as well as financial success, two of the most valued achievements in his Jewish culture. In all likelihood, he was well respected and influential in his community. He was probably the first in his class at the synagogue, the equivalent of the straight-A student, a teacher's dream. Success appears to have come easily for this seeker.

At the beginning of this account in Mark, the man introduced himself to Jesus by referring to him as "Good Teacher." In early Judaism, only God was referred to as good.[1] Either the young man addressed him this way because he saw Jesus as coming from God, or he was seeking to flatter Jesus, perhaps with the goal of Jesus reciprocating in kind. I am sure the young man was accustomed to being complimented for his many prior achievements.

His question for Jesus may have also indicated this need for affirmation. He asked Jesus, "What must I do to inherit eternal life?" If God's economy worked the same way as this young man's Jewish culture assumed it did, then he should have been in good standing for achieving this goal.[2] He should have been assured of eternal life, since God had apparently favored him in this earthly life. Wealth and other blessings in this temporal world were viewed by his contemporaries as proof that an individual pleased God. Poverty and illness were viewed as signs that an individual had failed to earn God's favor or had achieved favor but lost it at some point. This is why later in the account the disciples were amazed when Jesus stated that it was hard for the rich to enter the kingdom of God, asking Jesus, "Who then can be saved?" (Mark 10:23–26). It is also why in John's Gospel they asked, "Rabbi, who sinned, this man or his parents that he would be born blind?" before Jesus miraculously restored the man's sight (John 9:2). The prevailing cultural view was that any misfortune in life was deserved because of some prior sin committed either by the afflicted individuals or their ancestors.

This popular perception made Jesus' remarks in the Beatitudes, found in Matt 5:3–12, one of his most radical teachings. According to the prevailing belief, the poor would never inherit God's kingdom; the meek would never inherit the earth. Only the

1. Witherington, *Gospel of Mark*, 281.
2. Willard, *Divine Conspiracy*, 108.

strong and the wealthy could expect eternity in heaven. But Jesus challenged this assumption by including the poor, the cheated, and the suffering in his invitation to his kingdom.

Jesus' parable of the Pharisee and the Publican (Luke 18:9-14) reflected this same popular but mistaken view of God's favor in the attitudes expressed by each of the two characters. The Pharisee, confident of his own righteousness, thanked God that he was not like the poor tax collector and then listed two reasons as to why he deserved such status: his frequent fasting and his regular giving of alms to the poor. However, the tax collector understood his need for humility and begged for God's mercy. Those with the highest social status in this life expected to be at the top in the next life; those on the bottom rung had little hope of achieving eternal life. But Jesus assured his listeners that only the one who recognized his unworthiness would be justified before God—a radical contradiction to prevailing beliefs.

I believe the rich young ruler wanted Jesus to guarantee that if this man just continued doing what he was doing, heaven would be in his future. But Jesus didn't say this, because citizenship in his kingdom is not a result of what we do; it is a result of what he has done for us. Jesus did not tell the young man what he wanted to hear. The self-assured dream student had a weakness. He needed to be assured of his continued success.

## What do we know about Jesus from this interaction?

Jesus knew he was speaking with a well-educated, capable learner, so he answered the young man's initial question with one of his own, "Why do you call me good?" In Jesus' time, "good" only referred to one's ethical character rather than how well someone accomplished a task. We generally use the term "good teachers" as opposed to "poor teachers" when referring to their professional practice, not their moral character. But in his culture, the young man's use of the word was not a compliment on how well Jesus instructed; it was a comment on his being connected to the source of all goodness, God himself. It was an affirmation of Jesus' authority, expressed by the young man either because he genuinely believed this to be true or to gain favor with the remarkable teacher.

Of the three gospel passages that focus on this encounter, Mark's is the one I treasure most as an educator because of one particular verse. After the seeker tells Jesus that he has kept the law since he was a young boy, Mark writes in verse 10:21, "Jesus looked at him and loved him." I confess that I am tempted, at times, to respond to the overly-confident student with a comment or demand that would humble him or her a bit. I don't always have the purest of intentions when thinking of such comments, even if I delude myself into thinking it would be solely for the student's benefit. This is why I need verse 21. Even if the young man came across as arrogant or prideful, Jesus still loved him. Jesus knew his student's motivation, yet he responded with love.

Since Mark included this verse, we can be confident that Jesus' motive in asking the young man to give away his wealth was not because Christ despised rich individuals or that he resented the young man's arrogance. We can infer from verse 22 that this man treasured his possessions above everything else. According to Jesus, the man who had everything ironically lacked one thing. Christ understood that the man's self-perception was based upon his wealth, the most obvious sign of his success. The only way for this young ruler to transform his identity to that of a disciple was to remove this sign, so Jesus asked him to give it all away. But it must have been too high a price to pay for discipleship, since the young man sadly walked away.

## What can we learn from the rich young ruler?

One of the lessons we learn from this seeker is that there are no self-made men or women in the kingdom of heaven. I believe it is no coincidence that Mark records this account right after his narrative of Jesus blessing children (Mark 10:15–17). The juxtaposition of this interaction provides a contrast with the comments Jesus made about children:

## The Demanding Jesus and the Student Who Craved Success

> Let the little children come to me, and do not hinder them, for the kingdom of God belongs to such as these. Truly I tell you, anyone who does not receive the kingdom of God like a little child will never enter it. (Mark 10:16b–17)

Children are totally dependent on their caregivers. They trust and rely solely on their parents or guardians to provide what they need. Their survival is based on the relationship they have with their mother and father, not their own efforts. In the same way, we depend solely on what God, our Heavenly Father, has provided through his Son, Jesus. We cannot earn our way into heaven. All we can do is recognize that we are helpless outside of God's ability to redeem us.

I believe this was the stumbling block for the rich young ruler. He couldn't let go of his self-reliance. He couldn't let go of his legacy of success. I don't believe it was his actual wealth that prevented him from being a part of Christ's kingdom; it was the success and achievement it represented. Although the Apostle Paul shared a similar background and accomplishments, this young man could not give them up as Paul had:

> If someone else thinks they have reasons to put confidence in the flesh, I have more: circumcised on the eighth day, of the people of Israel, of the tribe of Benjamin, a Hebrew of Hebrews; in regard to the law, a Pharisee; as for zeal, persecuting the church; as for righteousness based on the law, faultless.
>
> But whatever were gains to me I now consider loss for the sake of Christ. What is more, I consider everything a loss because of the surpassing worth of knowing Christ Jesus my Lord, for whose sake I have lost all things. I consider them garbage that I may gain Christ. (Phil 3:4–8)

We also learn from the young man that our relationship with Christ cannot be a supplement to our efforts. We need to be "all in" or not at all. I believe the young man recognized that Jesus spoke truth to him, or he would have had a different reaction to

Christ's demand. He would have argued with Jesus about his assignment rather than resigning himself to his inability to fulfill it. Mark writes that "he sadly walked away." Unlike most of the interactions Jesus has in the gospel accounts, this time we are left with an unhappy ending.

One of the common elements between this young man's worldview and that of contemporary American culture is the bifurcation he made between being good and leading the good life. More specifically, it is the difference between leading "the good life" and leading *a* good life. One involves pursuit of pleasure, while the other involves the pursuit of morality. This young man would probably have seen himself as a good person—one who led an obedient, godly life—but it came at no personal cost to his lifestyle.

Ask someone today to identify a good person, and he or she would probably name Mother Teresa. She was a person our society admired for her self-sacrificing commitment to poor and dying souls in India. But in our culture, as was true for the young man, leading a good life is not something we necessarily all want to emulate. Not many of us would choose Mother Teresa's life of service in the streets of Calcutta as our life's work. Like the young ruler, we prefer the comforts and security of wealth and the prestige of influence, rather than the humility and poverty of Mother Teresa's missionary service. Like the rich young ruler, we also face the challenge of living a sacrificial life.

## What can we learn from Jesus in this interaction?

Jesus recognized that his student was well-educated and confident, so he used a different approach than he used with individuals who were physically hurting or socially marginalized. He challenged the young man and clearly answered his question of what was required to earn eternal life. He made no attempt to compromise his requirement for kingdom citizenship. And his assignment was final. He made no modifications, nor did he relax his due date.

Although Jesus' response was harsh, we must be careful of what Jesus did not say in this interaction. Willard points out that Scripture does not teach that wealth is evil in and of itself.[3] It is the love of money that is sinful (1 Tim 6:10). However, Jesus himself warns his followers about the futility of storing up treasures on earth in Matt 6:19 and about the deceitfulness of wealth in Mark 4:19. We cannot make attaining riches and the power and influence they typically bring our life's goal. But this is not to say God cannot use wealthy individuals in his kingdom. The work of the global church has been accomplished, in part, due to the significant resources of past and current generous followers of Christ. Like all talents, the ability to earn and grow capital can be used for selfish purposes or for the kingdom of God.

The irony of salvation in Christ is that it is freely given, but it demands everything. Although it is not earned, it requires total transformation. It turns most of our prior values upside down. This was the lesson Jesus had for the young ruler, and it is the same lesson for all of us.

Another lesson that we learn from Jesus in this interaction is that whatever you have done in your past, it doesn't matter. This is freeing for individuals whose past is filled with regret; they are released of their burden through Christ's forgiveness. But it is threatening for individuals with a self-perceived stellar track record. This chapter of Mark concludes with Jesus' words about eternal life, "Many who are first will be last, and the last first" (Mark 10:31). God's kingdom values offer great comfort to those who have failed, but they can be very troubling to those who have been successful like the rich young ruler.

## What can we, as educators, learn from this interaction?

I believe novice teachers are some of the most optimistic people in the world. They may get overwhelmed by the enormity of

---

3. Willard, *Divine Conspiracy*, 108.

their professional responsibilities, but they believe that, despite circumstances, all of their students can grow in knowledge and understandings that will improve their lives. These young educators are dedicated to enabling their students to be successful. This commitment requires these teachers to provide accommodations or differentiated assignments in order to ensure that all learning targets are accessible to every learner.

Although this belief that every student can achieve a learning target is significantly motivating to educators, it can be detrimental as well. As a supervisor of student teachers, I often need to remind my novices to stop reviewing a unit's material and give the summative assessment even though not every student may have mastered its content. My pre-service teachers frequently want to wait until they are confident that every student will "ace" the exam. However, experienced teachers know that providing the opportunity to learn content and mastering that content are not synonymous. The former is solely the teacher's responsibility, while the latter is a responsibility shared with the learner. A teacher could wait until the school year ends to assess a continuously instructed concept, but it may still be that not every student will have mastered it by that time. As educators, we know that we are required to assess and move on, but we want the happy Hollywood ending every time. We don't want anyone to fail because we perceive that it indicates we too have failed.

But Jesus let his student fail. He let the rich young ruler walk away.

Because of our commitment to every student's success, I think teachers, more than any other group, find the ending of Jesus' lesson for the rich young ruler shocking. It goes against everything we want for our students. It leaves us so unsettled because we never learn whether this young man ultimately does what Christ asks him to do in order to follow him.

When I read this encounter, I have to say honestly that I would never have done what Jesus did. I would have run after the young man and stopped him and said, "Wait up! What about first giving just half of your fortune away? Could you do that? If not, then what about trying a third?"

I would have reduced the assignment to avoid harming my relationship with the student. That way, I would have seen some measure of success, and in doing so, I would have felt good about the outcome, limited as it was. This would be a dangerous instructional path. Offering this option would reveal that my sense of self-worth as a teacher is more important to me than the damage my compromise could cause the student. I would not be speaking truth to the young man as Jesus did. I would really be putting my need to be successful ahead of everything else. In doing this, I would have cheated my student.

All children and adolescents, no matter what their abilities, interests, or prior experience level, no matter what the content, need to learn that they are responsible for their own learning. One of the biggest lessons I had to learn as a novice teacher was not to equate understanding my student with excusing my student. So even though life at home may have been difficult for one of my students, I could not excuse him from turning in his homework. I may have needed to modify an assignment for my student with a learning disability, but I still needed to insist she finish it. Even if the student's view of me changed, I still had to hold him or her responsible for following through on a requirement. Repeatedly offering my misguided "grace" would communicate that I saw them as incapable of meeting my expectations. This could lead them to develop a sense of "learned helplessness,"[4] a state where students do not see themselves as having the capacity to meet their responsibilities. This results in a loss of agency. In doing this, I would have cheated these students of learning the important life skill of being responsible as well as learning an academic one.

When we apply this ill-fitting mind-set of extending excuses instead of understanding toward groups of individuals, it becomes a negative stereotype that diminishes their achievement and ultimately damages our relationship with them. Although stereotyping can occasionally lead to an individual child from an accomplished

4. Seligman, *Learned Optimism*, 15.

family being held to an unrealistic standard, most often it fosters a deficit model perspective by which we only see students for what they lack rather than what they have to offer. Historically, these "excuses" have led to gross educational inequities in terms of access to resources and quality instruction. Over time, these inequities in our nation have led to disparities in employment, income, rates of incarceration, and health.

Author of *The Dreamkeepers: Successful Teachers of African American Children*,[5] Gloria Ladson-Billings refers to these chronic and pervasive inequities as the "achievement debt," which is conceptually similar to the financial burden of our national debt. When asked what she wished every teacher or community member knew about this achievement debt, she responded, "Despite what it looks like, students show up with incredible strengths and assets. Kids are capable of much more than we think, and right now our expectations are being set way too low."[6]

Teachers who maintain high standards for their students create an ethos of significant achievement. I witnessed this during a literacy lesson in an urban, linguistically and ethnically diverse fifth-grade classroom. I must admit that when I first saw the learning target written on the whiteboard, "Students will define and identify the motif in a novel," I doubted all students could achieve it. Although I predicted that the on-level readers in my student teacher's class could attain this goal, I questioned whether students at this age but reading two grades below level could fully understand such an abstract concept.

My student teacher first defined the term and then inductively taught the concept from an anchor novel her class had just finished, with individual students supplying examples of the concept from the familiar text. She then assigned her six "book clubs" the task of collaboratively identifying the motif from their various novels, requiring them to back up their claim with textual evidence. After twenty minutes of small-group discussions, the six groups of fifth-graders reported their findings. I was not surprised

---

5. See Ladson-Billings, *Dreamkeepers*.
6. Ladson-Billings, "Q & A with Gloria Ladson-Billings," 1.

by the level of thinking from her students who read at or above grade level, but I was amazed by her below-level literacy group's reading of E. B. White's *Charlotte's Web*, a third-grade-level chapter book. They reported back that they had determined the motif of *Charlotte's Web* to be the web itself, since through it everyone learned the famous pig, Wilbur's, value. They then cited several passages in the book that proved their theory.

Similarly, I was surprised by the depth of thinking from my student teacher's second group, which had read Beverly Cleary's fourth-grade-level chapter book, *Henry and Ribsy*. They identified its motif as being lost because not only was Ribsy the dog lost in the book, his owner, Henry, was somewhat lost too. They also supplied strong textual evidence to prove their hypothesis.

Because of my student teacher and her mentor's high expectations and careful planning, every student in their class achieved a highly abstract and challenging learning goal, including their students with an Individualized Education Program (IEP), English learners, and those who could not read grade-level materials. Over 93 percent of students in this school were identified as low-income, but all their fifth grade students accomplished the learning target. Together these teachers made a challenging concept accessible to students at different reading levels by first enabling and then expecting every student to meet the same requirement. These educators did not compromise, because they perceived every learner to be competent for the task. Their students completed the full requirements of the assignment not only because they were able to understand the concept involved, but because they also knew that failing to complete all aspects of the task would be viewed as unacceptable by their teachers.

Jesus demonstrated two significant mind-sets for teachers in this passage. Not only did he see his learner as competent to meet his expectation, he also allowed his student to suffer the consequences of failing to reach it. This second principle is by far the more difficult one for beginning teachers. It is tempting to over-identify with a student's failure and blame outside factors, including ourselves, for his or her lack of success. But when we do this, we teach an unintended but dangerous lesson that diminishes our student's sense of agency and accountability.

We learn important truths from Jesus and the rich young ruler that have an impact on our professional as well as spiritual lives. To teach like a disciple, we cannot compromise our expectations.

4

# The Holistic Jesus and the Student Who Needed Healing

## *Mark 5:24-34*

IN THIS CHAPTER, we will focus on Jesus' brief interaction with a student who is unnamed, yet who is so representative of Jesus' care and power that all three Synoptic Gospel authors record her story. She is known most frequently as "the woman who touched Jesus' garment." Her encounter with Jesus is actually an interruption in another story—the healing of Jairus' daughter. Both Jairus and this woman had a common request of Jesus—miraculous physical healing. Jairus, a synagogue leader, risked his professional and personal reputation by asking the controversial Jesus to come to his home in order to cure his twelve-year-old child. Jesus promised to come, but on the way, he encountered a woman who was also in need of his healing touch.

### What do we know about this woman?

The account, found in Matt 9:20-22, Mark 5:24-34, and Luke 8:42-48, is quite descriptive of the woman's background and her unusual character, considering that all three authors relate such a brief interaction. We learn she had hemorrhaged for twelve years and that she had spent all her resources seeking medical help from many physicians. At the point when she met Jesus, however, her condition was worse than before she began her treatment. She could easily have been anemic by this point in her life due to the long-term pattern of continuous bleeding she had experienced.

Not only was the woman affected physically, but being Jewish, her illness also carried social and religious repercussions as well. Old Testament law placed significant restrictions on a woman during her monthly menstrual period. Leviticus 15:19–24 stated that a menstruating Jewish woman was impure for seven days each month. Anyone who touched her directly would become similarly unclean. Women remained close to home during this period because anyone touching the furniture she sat upon would also become unclean. Jewish women and anyone in contact with them were required to follow specific procedures for washing and sacrificing in order to be restored to community life and worship after these seven days.

This particular woman's illness may or may not have been related to her menstrual cycle, but Lev 15:25–30 outlines the identical procedure for a woman who bleeds from other causes. She had to wait a certain period of time after the bleeding stopped and then follow the same purifying ritual. Either way, she had been ceremonially unclean for the entire twelve years of her condition. Although being unclean was not the same as being sinful, anyone who did not strictly follow the Leviticus guidelines was considered sinful. As a result, she was in a long-standing, legally-imposed time of isolation. Her illness carried with it a social and spiritual cost as well as a physical toll.

Because of her chronic and pervasive condition, she was penniless, probably pitied, and perhaps even ostracized from her community. She certainly had to have withdrawn from public life, but she somehow heard of Jesus' reputation for healing and developed a secretive plan to meet him. According to Mark's account, her hope was to blend in with the crowd, approach him from behind, touch his cloak, and quietly disappear again into the crowd. Her desire was that no one would ever learn she was there.

We know from Jesus' comments later in the story that her plan was based on her firm conviction that he could cure her. She did not venture out with a "What have I got to lose?"-level of motivation. Her faith in Jesus did not even require him to engage her in conversation; merely touching his clothes would be sufficient to cure her. In fact, she hoped she would not have to say anything to him. Her desire was to move in, solve her problem, and move on. She wanted to remain invisible.

Both Jairus, the father of the dying girl, and this woman took great risks due to the desperate states in which they found themselves. Even though he jeopardized losing the respect of his professional community for contacting Jesus, Jairus had no other choice. Like many other parents, I have stood in his shoes, knowing what it's like to hear that your child has been diagnosed with a grave and often fatal illness. I know firsthand that all other concerns pale in light of finding a means to your daughter's full recovery. This sick woman risked facing an equally ostracizing community by venturing out into public. Even worse, she risked the anger of the healer whose help she sought. She could only imagine what his rebuke might be if he realized that she had made him and every other person in the crowd unclean because of her actions. Her goal of physical healing could result in further and permanent rejection from her people. The potential harm that could result from her plan was enormous.

I am a lot like the woman who sought healing. Although I would never call myself a serious risk-taker, I develop prayers a lot like the woman's plan. I move in with my list of requests, expect Jesus to solve my problems, and then move on with the rest of my life until the next crisis develops. In fact, the more I examine my prayer life, the more the comparison fits me. I outline exactly Jesus' role for my struggle, even to the point of trying to define his relationship with me. In effect, I specifically tell him what to do to fix my troubling circumstances. Not only is this arrogant, it also makes Jesus' role so much smaller in my life than he desires and deserves. Nowhere in Isa 9:6 is the promised Messiah called Personal Problem-Solver. He is referred to as the Prince of Peace, Mighty God, and Wonderful Counselor but never Mr. Fix-It. The sick woman merely wanted Jesus to heal her, but he chose instead to transform her and her community.

## What do we know about Jesus from this interaction?

As with lepers and the Samaritan woman at the well, Jesus seemed to have little concern for social or religious convention here. He engaged with anyone who sought his help, no matter where they fit into the social structure of the day. He never appeared to be afraid of ruining his reputation with Israel's elite. His role in the story began when the sick woman had nearly accomplished her purpose. She moved in close to Jesus, touched him, experienced his healing power, and was edging out of the crowd when Jesus interrupted her escape. If he worried about embarrassing her or himself, he would have let her leave him quietly. However, Jesus had a bigger goal to accomplish.

I find it fascinating that Mark states that while Jesus was aware that power had gone out from him, he doesn't quite say that Jesus was surprised by it. We get a glimpse of the interplay of his human nature and his divine nature in this story. Jesus was immediately aware that someone had been healed by merely touching him. I wonder if he felt a drain on his power or just a difference. I realize that Jesus is God and not a fictional superhero, but his awareness that he could heal without conscious effort is an amazing aspect of his divinity. He turned around and asked, "Who touched my clothes?"

I do enjoy the role of the disciples in this report. As in several other encounters, they play the role of the straight man here. Perhaps a bit sarcastically, they answered, "You see the people crowding against you and yet you can ask, 'Who touched me?'" They are the linear, literal thinkers of their day—a role that often prevents us from seeing God at work. I appreciate the honesty of the gospel writers so much because had I been one of the twelve disciples, I would have requested that the author edit that question from the story to make us look less imperceptive. Their refusal to make themselves look more astute attests to the truth of Scripture. The chosen twelve were willing to tell the account without any spin on it so that the truth of Christ's identity would be revealed. They did not mind looking foolish if it made the revelation more accurate.

Jesus then took the time to look through the crowd for the woman. But at the same time, Jesus was not alone. At this point, Jairus was probably standing next to Jesus looking at the sun to see how late it was, wondering why he was wasting precious time. This woman's crisis was over, but his was yet to be resolved. How could Christ stop to talk with this woman when his daughter was dying? Jairus must have been frantic. I know I would have been upset with Jesus for stopping to converse in this moment.

Jairus was not the only one who was anxious. The woman, "trembling with fear," turned back, fell at Jesus' feet, and recounted her story to him. Mark states she "told him the whole truth." She had no idea what the outcome of her confession might be. What judgment might she receive from the healer? Would he return her to her previous condition? Would he banish her for being deceitful? But at the conclusion of her testimony, Jesus told her, "Daughter, your faith has healed you. Go in peace, and be freed from your suffering."

How was Jesus' pronouncement different from his physical act of healing her? I believe this statement is the key to his relationship with her. She wanted only physical healing. She would have gladly settled for it if Jesus had let her carry out her escape. But then she would have only been cured of her illness. Jesus sought to heal her holistically. By drawing attention to her physical change, he restored her socially as well. Her community was now witness to the physical transformation in her body. She would not be marginalized any longer.

By proclaiming that her faith had healed her, Jesus also restored her spiritually. He affirmed her belief and, in doing this, instructed his disciples and the crowd on the greater importance of faith over works. Her restoration was not a result of following the law. She was freed from her suffering because of grace, not justice. For the first time in twelve years, she found peace and freedom from her suffering. This would not have been possible without Jesus making her very private miracle public.

## What can we learn from this woman and from Jairus?

Mark continues the story with messengers bringing the news that Jairus' daughter had died. It appeared that Jesus was too late to fulfill the father's request. But Jesus ignored the message and told Jairus not to be afraid but only to believe. They arrived at the house and, finding the funeral lament already started, Jesus assured the mourners that the girl was only sleeping. He entered the home, took her hand, called her by name to wake up, and then raised her from the dead. Again, Jesus resisted social and religious convention by touching the deceased girl's hand—another means of becoming unclean.

Both individuals in this account, Jairus and the woman, had incredible faith. The circumstances surrounding their crises demonstrated an utterly unreasonable faith, but they believed in Jesus' power and authority regardless of the situation. How could touching the hem of a healer's robe do more than years of treatment from doctors? How could a daughter who had already died be brought back to full health? Jairus and the sick woman may have been at opposite ends of society's spectrum, but they both chose faith over the facts of their case.

As mentioned before, these two individuals took an incredible risk to seek out Jesus' help. But before healing had fully occurred, Jesus elevated their risk. By calling the woman out, he required her to make her story public. By waiting until Jairus' daughter had expired, he insisted that the father trust him beyond any reasonable hope. Because of Jesus' demands, both of them also realized that they needed more than healing; they needed a relationship with the healer.

## What can we learn from Jesus in this interaction?

The first lesson we learn from Jesus' relationship with the sick woman is the importance of faith. Hebrews 11:6 states, "Without faith it is impossible to please God, because anyone who comes to him must believe that he exists and that he rewards those who seek him." This truth was embodied in the lives of the sick woman, Jairus, and Jesus himself. Our relationship with him is dependent on our faith in who he is and what he has done for us.

The second lesson we learn is that Jesus wants to restore us holistically. In many ways this story, while true, is a metaphor for Christ's redemptive work on Calvary. I recall as a child asking to wash the living room floor of my grandparents' summer cottage when we opened it up one spring. After my mother handed me a bucket of soapy water and a clean rag, I began to scrub in earnest. I was therefore incredibly surprised some thirty minutes later when she walked into the room to inspect my work and laughed rather than commending me on my efforts. She noticed that while I had remembered to reach every corner, I had failed to change the water when it became dirty. I ended up merely transferring the dirt from one part of the floor to another. I didn't realize that my soapy water would become ineffective over time. It needed to be replenished in order to clean the entire floor.

There is a saying that for something to become clean, something else must become dirty. A clean floor is only possible if a rag and pail of water become soiled. The only way a greasy window becomes clean again is for a paper towel to end up wearing the grime.

In the same way, the only way the woman could become clean was to make Jesus unclean. That's true for all of us. Second Corinthians 5:21 states, "God made him who had no sin to be sin for us, so that in him we might become the righteousness of God." He was willing to take on this horrendous burden so that we could be redeemed and would thereby find freedom from our sin. Because of Christ, we also can "go in peace and be freed from our suffering."

Finally from this account, we also learn that Jesus' priorities are often different from our own or what we think his priorities should be. The sick woman would have been content to have him merely solve her problem, but he wanted to change her life. The father wanted his daughter healed, but Jesus raised her to full health from the dead. His interest in us is far greater than merely answering our requests or fixing our problems. He wants to transform our lives too. Allowing him to fulfill his purposes in our lives, rather than our own plans, also requires faith.

## What can we, as educators, learn from this interaction?

Although teachers are not healers, they share many of the same roles as physicians. Just as doctors diagnose and develop treatment plans for their patients, teachers similarly diagnose causes for a student's inability to learn. They construct an educational plan that uses specific strategies to capitalize on a student's strengths or compensate for a student's weakness. Teachers then measure growth to determine if a given method is effective for a student in the same way that the medical profession assesses a patient's progress to decide if a particular treatment is working.

However, teachers do more than correct academic weaknesses. Teachers who pattern their lives after Christ view their work as much more than adding a year's academic growth to students' achievement levels. They view their students as whole individuals—as academic, physical, emotional, social, moral, and spiritual beings. Not every student will shine in a classroom, but teachers must be serious talent scouts, seeking out students' strengths wherever they may lie. They do this not only to find an avenue for greater academic success, but also to understand and value their individual students as human beings. Children are image-bearers of God, no matter what their test scores may be.

I recall getting to know a young kindergartner who was enrolled in my child's class and was significantly challenged in staying on task. He had a full-time aide assigned to keep him on track for instruction. Every day, his classmates waited for him to focus on instruction or join them in their activities. He had a sweet disposition, but often his behavior had a negative impact on the other students. Throughout both semesters, I observed the patience of his teacher, his aide, and his peers. They were witness to all the struggles he had with paying attention in the classroom. His behavior affected him in and out of the classroom. Field trips were rather tense, as this young boy wandered off whenever he was not closely watched.

At the end of the year, his mother sent birthday party invitations to every child in his class. The celebration was held at a local ice-skating rink. Even though we already had an event planned for that day, I made certain that my child attended the party. I was concerned that few students would choose to participate because of the continuous stress this child's learning challenges had created for his peers.

Fortunately, many children did attend the celebration. It was comical to see these five- and six-year-olds wobble on the ice; for many, including my daughter, it was their first time lacing up skates. They spent much of the hour "walking" on the ice, carefully clutching the railing that surrounded the rink.

The birthday boy, however, was amazing. He skated forward and backward with ease, spinning with grace and wonderful control. He was an absolute star on the ice. All the parents attending the party were stunned at his skill and confidence and so grateful that their children could see him in his element.

I was struck by two thoughts. First, I wished the young boy had an October birthday rather than May so that his classmates could have seen his competence much earlier in their relationships with him. Second, I realized how limiting the "show and tell" arena is for many young learners. There are no ice rinks in elementary school classrooms; there are few venues where children whose talents exist outside of academics can "shine." Perceptive teachers need to discover these areas of strength and highlight them.

Jesus perceived this strength in the sick woman. He saw her for more than her illness. He saw her as a brave, faith-filled woman risking everything because of her belief in his ability to heal her. He not only restored her as a complete individual, he also perceived her as one. In this way, he was an exemplary model of best practice.

I teach classes in a four-year liberal arts college. Every year a fair number of our alumni return at Homecoming, but I am quite certain that none of my former students has ever come back to campus for the purpose of reviewing the academic content I had taught them in one of my courses. I hope they have applied the content we covered in their professional practice, but it is not the content that endears students to a teacher, professor, or school community. It is the relationships they form there with faculty, staff, and other students. Our connections are grounded in relationship, in recognizing and valuing each other.

One of the unique aspects of the relationships that teachers form with their students is that it is not only based on who their students are at the present time, but also on who they are becoming. My students, whether they are at the kindergarten or graduate level, will become professionals, homemakers, parents, citizens, athletes, volunteers, spouses, and church members. These roles will require a variety of skills, far more than academic ones. This holistic view of learners—seeing them both now as complete individuals and who they will be in adult life—is critical to helping students develop into competent, mature human beings.

Not only is this professional mind-set biblically based, it is also an important component of educational research. Nel Noddings raises the question of why we do not focus more of the curriculum on these more holistic life skills:

> Today we insist that everyone (almost without exception) study academic mathematics. Yet relatively few students will actually use this material in their adult lives. In contrast all of us will make a home of some sort. Why then does homemaking not appear as a serious and sustained subject in our schools?[1]

We all know of at least one individual whose academic career was stellar yet whose home life was miserable. And we also know of individuals whose academic careers were weak but whose relational, organizational, and parenting abilities were such that they had a rich and rewarding personal life. Few educators notice these abilities, let alone affirm them or develop them in all students.

Another lesson we can learn from this biblical account is that Jesus was not reluctant to push his students. He raised the level of

---

1. Noddings, *Critical Lessons*, 6.

risk for both Jairus and the sick woman in order to develop their faith. Concepts, skills, or dispositions need to be accessible, but they should not be reduced to their simplest form. Engagement always requires an appropriate level of challenge. Too often, students fail to connect with the learning process or subject matter. Klem and Connell found that "by high school as many as forty per cent to sixty per cent of students become chronically disengaged from school."[2]

In retrospect, learners tend to value the difficult journey over the easy one. When asked what they appreciated most about working with our college orchestra conductor, one of his musicians replied, "We first read through a difficult piece that we all think we will never be able to play, but then he gets us to the point where we not only can play it, we can't wait to perform it." Although the task must be ultimately doable, mastering something difficult brings a sense of accomplishment that completing simple or routine assignments do not. The challenge for all educators is finding the right levels of rigor to enable students at various experience levels to invest their time and intellectual effort.

Sullivan and Lilburn encourage elementary mathematics teachers to develop their students' critical and creative thinking by rephrasing their simple questions to more complex ones. One of their examples involves transforming the basic recall question, "What is the average of . . . ?" into "What five numbers could we average to make 13?"[3] Even though the second question is more difficult, it is more inviting for elementary students at differing levels of expertise, particularly advanced students who might offer fractions, decimals, or negative integers in their series of addends.

These important lessons on requiring rigor and developing our ability to see students from a broader perspective are learned from Jesus and the woman who touched his garment. To teach like a disciple, we need to recognize our students' full range of talents and then challenge our students to grow in all aspects of life.

---

2. Klem and Connell, "Relationships Matter," 262.
3. Sullivan and Lilburn, *Good Questions*, 4.

5

# The Multicultural Jesus and the Student Who Needed Acceptance

## John 4:3–42

JESUS' INTERACTION WITH THE Samaritan woman, found in John 4:3–42, could be re-titled "Jesus and the Other" because you cannot find an encounter with an individual more dissimilar from Jesus than the woman he met outside the town of Sychar at Jacob's well. She differed from him by ethnicity, gender, social status, and experience. Jesus' ability to relate to her despite these contrasts has much to teach us about educating those whose backgrounds are unlike our own.

Research supports the theory that without intervention, instructors tend to teach in the way that they themselves learn best.[1] This tendency results in instructors being more effective in teaching students whose backgrounds and experiences most closely mirror their own. Professional educators, however, are charged with creating instructional environments that meet the learning needs of all their students. In order to do this, they need to switch their focus from teacher-centered instruction to learner-focused instruction. Jesus showed us a great example of this practice in his encounter with the Samaritan woman.

In this interaction, Jesus meets a woman by Jacob's well after sending his disciples into town to buy food. He is tired and thirsty, so he engages the woman by first asking her for a drink. The conversation that follows moves on to spiritual matters, comparing

---

1. Stitt-Gohdes, "Student Teachers," 22.

physical water to the living water Jesus offers. He displays supernatural insight as he establishes a relationship with the woman, revealing his knowledge of her past as well as making the claim that he is the Messiah. Jesus' manner and teaching amazes her to the point of prompting her to call others from her village to meet him and hear his message.

## What do we know about the Samaritan woman?

This woman was a Samaritan, a group that had long received hostility from the Jews. The Jews regarded them as ethnically and spiritually impure because they had intermarried with their captors, established a different place of worship, and recognized only the Pentateuch—the first five books of the Old Testament—as their Scriptures.[2] Jews avoided speaking with Samaritans, often taking a longer route around that geographic area to avoid interacting with them. Jewish men also were not to speak with women who were unfamiliar to them, so by merely asking this woman for a drink, Jesus broke with two social conventions of his culture.

It was therefore not surprising that the woman questioned Jesus' request. Why would he, a Jew, ask her for a drink? Samaritan women were particularly ostracized by Jewish men. If the biblical reference to the sixth hour refers to noon, this woman went to get her water during the warmest part of the day, the time when no one else was likely to be drawing water. Her timing may be an indication that the woman was also ostracized by her own community. Later in the account when Jesus asks her to go and bring her husband, we find out that she had five previous husbands and was now living with a sixth man. Her frequent marriages and current relationship could not have earned her respect within her community. Because of this, she may have avoided speaking with others in her town and therefore found Jesus' question all the more surprising.

2. Goldsmith, *Jesus and His Relationships*, 76.

If the sixth hour refers to six hours after noon, then it would explain Jesus' fatigue, but this raises the question of why the Samaritan woman would need to go into the village to bring back other members of her community. One would expect others to be getting water at this time. Either way, neither she nor Jesus conversed with anyone else who may have been at the well. Perhaps she seldom engaged with anyone in conversation.

We also learn from Jesus' offer of living water that this woman was knowledgeable. She understood the history of her people, stating their relationship to Jacob and their contrasting theological views with Jews. She was also intelligent enough to infer that Jesus was speaking prophetically and then drew the conclusion that he himself must be a prophet. She had to have been theologically educated to be aware of the coming Messiah. The issues they discussed were far more substantive than typical "water cooler" conversation.

Finally, we know from this passage that she was courageous. She took a risk by responding to Jesus. She could have ignored him or quickly given him his water and left the well. But she chose instead to stay and talk with him. Even when Jesus revealed her past to her, she did not leave out of fear or embarrassment. Then when the disciples returned and nonverbally communicated their surprise at seeing Jesus speak with her, she did not retreat. When she did leave the well without her water jar, it was to gather her community and return with them to meet this amazing Jesus. If she had previously been shunned by her fellow citizens, she showed remarkable bravery in this action as well.

## What do we know about Jesus from this interaction?

The first characteristic of Jesus that we gain from this passage is the fact that he was fully human. He was tired and thirsty as a result of his journey. The disciples had been sent to purchase food, and their comments to him when they returned acknowledged that Jesus had to be hungry as well. He experienced the same physical needs for food and rest that all of us experience.

## Jesus and the Student Who Needed Acceptance

Second, we see that Jesus perceived the difference between what is important and what is irrelevant. He disregarded the social customs of his day in order to speak with the Samaritan woman. This action demonstrates that Jesus valued the individual over his own reputation. We know from John's account that the disciples were surprised by his action of speaking with her even though they said nothing. This was not the only occasion when Jesus amazed them with his behavior. The gospels record several events in which Jesus had conflicts with the Pharisees because he ignored cultural conventions in order to do his more important work. Some of these disagreements centered on his healing on the Sabbath (Luke 13:10-17), calling a tax-collector as his disciple (Luke 5:27-32), and refraining from the practice of fasting (Luke 5:33-39). As when speaking with the Samaritan woman at Jacob's well, Jesus paid little attention to these customs, choosing instead to focus his actions and teaching on his larger purpose, which was to do the work of his Father.

Finally, we see evidence of Jesus' divinity in this account. His ability to identify the woman's past and current background and, more significantly, his revelation that he was the very Messiah that she had named pointed to his godly nature. She recognized that he was unlike anyone she had ever known, possessing an insight that was beyond mere human understanding. Because of this revelation, she invited everyone from her community to grasp that he was "the Savior of the world" (John 4:42).

### What can we learn from the Samaritan woman?

First, the woman learned that her past did not determine her future. For a woman whose numerous marriages probably lowered her social status in earthly life, she was not destined to fail in receiving eternal life. Becoming a part of God's family was nothing she had to earn; it was personally offered as a gift from Jesus. This truth must have brought her incredible joy. Jesus offers this same good news to us. Our past does not determine our future in Jesus' kingdom.

Second, the woman allowed the truth of Jesus' message to transform her life. She could have become defensive when he confronted her with the truth about her current life situation. Instead, she listened and believed. Meeting Jesus and realizing his identity was such an amazing encounter that it transformed her relationships with others. She went back to her village announcing, "Come see a man who told me everything I ever did. Could this be the Messiah?" (John 4:29). As a result of her invitation, many residents of Sychar believed and asked Jesus to stay there with them for a few days in order to teach them. By this action, she is also a good example to us of sharing the good news of the Messiah with others.

## What can we learn from Jesus in this interaction?

The first thing we learn from Jesus is that he was not afraid of appearing vulnerable. By this I mean that he needed something, and he was not too proud to ask for the woman's help, even for a cup of water. He did not alter his plans because of social convention or his disciples' unspoken criticism for disregarding it. His mission and love for others always transcended the circumstances surrounding an individual or social issue.

Even more important than his attitude was Jesus' purpose in asking the woman for help. His request for water showed her his respect and recognition that she had something to offer him. He leveled the playing field, so to speak. Rather than regarding the woman as someone unworthy of his time and conversation, he turned to her as a resource. Engaging her in a substantive conversation after the drink confirmed this to her even more. It signified that Jesus valued her for more than meeting his need for water. He saw her for her capabilities rather than her deficiencies. I believe this is what made such a lasting impression on her. His insights into her past may have required divine ability, but she never would have stayed long enough to hear them if he had not connected with her first on this very human level. Although Jesus recognized the differences between their cultures, he saw her as being part of a larger culture—as a member of the entire human family he had come to rescue. Through the metaphor of living water, he invited her to become a part of his redeemed kingdom.

Jesus was able to transcend all the categories that separated him from the Samaritan woman. His regard for her as a person cut across gender, ethnic, social class, and theological boundaries. He helped the woman and subsequent generations of believers who read John's Gospel to see that where one worshipped—a huge dividing line between Judaism and Samaritan theology—was not as important as the mind-set behind how one worshipped. Another lesson found in his conversation was that following minor religious rules was not as important as recognizing our need for salvation and the One who provides it for us. This cornerstone truth of the gospels unifies all Christ's followers.

Finally, the most significant lesson we learn from Jesus and the Samaritan woman is that Jesus accepts all who genuinely seek him, no matter what they have experienced in their past. Our history never disqualifies us from his invitation. No matter what we have done, experienced, or endured, we are never beyond his grace and forgiveness. We have the assurance of eternity with him because he offers these same gifts to us. This truth is our ultimate hope.

This truth, however, is also our challenge. Our goal should be to see others the same way Jesus sees them. We need to recognize others as individuals created in God's image, see them for their abilities and not their deficits, and focus on what we have in common with them rather than how they are different from us so we can make that human connection necessary for establishing a relationship. We are challenged to extend warmth to them in the same way that Jesus extended an invitation to the woman he met at the well. She expected him to reject her, but instead she found his welcome.

## What can we, as educators, learn from this interaction?

The 2014–2015 academic year marked a tipping point in public education. For the first time, minority students outnumbered white students by 50.3 percent to 49.7 percent.[3] The growing U.S. minority population, which is expected to surpass the white population by 2043, results in every classroom becoming increasingly racially, linguistically, theologically, socially, and economically diverse. Elementary and secondary schools within my district serve families that speak over sixty different languages at home. Additionally, a federal education policy of inclusion brings a wide range of students who are eligible for special education services into the regular classroom. Teachers must be prepared to differentiate their instruction in order to meet students' broad span of linguistic, academic, and social needs. This task may appear overwhelming at times, since these students require different entrance points to any given learning task and may need varying levels of support to complete it. It can be tempting to see students' differences merely as obstacles to learning or problems to be solved.

Just as Jesus saw the Samaritan woman's characteristics as a means to developing a relationship with her, we need to see our diverse students' characteristics as the starting point to making connections with them. This is not to ignore the challenges that accompany teaching a child whose first language is not English or a student who has a developmental disability, but it requires a conscious decision not to define these individuals by such distinctions. A child is much more than her level of English proficiency and so much more than his learning disability. Parker Palmer reminds us that as human beings, we have much more in common with our most diverse students than we have differences. But he also reminds us that we share a responsibility in relating to these differences:

> In a pluralistic society, the way to truth is to listen attentively to diverse voices and views for the claims they

3. Maxwell, "U.S. School Enrollment," 14.

## Jesus and the Student Who Needed Acceptance

make on us. The bond of listening holds the cosmic community together—careful vulnerable listening for how things look from this standpoint and that and that, a listening not only to know the other but to be known from the other's point of view.[4]

I once asked a cooperating teacher how her instructional role had changed as a result of a large number of Rwandan refugee children enrolling in her predominantly white, middle-class school that year. She responded that she and her entire fourth grade class had been enriched by two orphaned twin brothers who had arrived mid-semester. She recalled when, on the first day after winter break, many of her other students had entered her classroom talking about their Christmas presents, complaining a bit of how they had wanted several particular video games but had only gotten "this one" or "that one." To help them get past their holiday experiences and refocus on learning, she asked each child to share their favorite gift. A lot of video games were mentioned until the two boys shared. Both of the twin brothers, who were now being raised by an aunt and uncle, beamed as one shared that he had received oranges and the other shared that he had received a shirt.

My friend said their conversation was transformative. All the talk of disappointment with Christmas presents vanished as the rest of her students absorbed what the boys were saying. "We all learned so much more from these boys than I ever taught them. By their words and their attitude, they taught us to be grateful for things we all took for granted," she concluded.

As a result of her interactions with these boys, she loved having refugee students in her class each year. She saw them not for the prior learning experiences they lacked but for what their presence added to everyone's learning experience. This teacher not only viewed her diverse students as assets in her class, she also modeled this perception to her other students. She wanted her class to look past appearances and connect with these brothers as regular fourth graders, learning from their individual interests and talents as well as from their prior experiences.

4. Palmer, *To Know as We Are Known*, 67.

In offering a glimmer of hope for our country's current state of race relations, *Chicago Tribune* columnist Heidi Stevens wrote of a conversation with her daughter who attends a Chicago public school:

> At the beginning of her second-grade year, my daughter was filling out a questionnaire for school when she stumbled on a question she couldn't answer. "Which most closely describes you: white, black, Latino, Pacific Islander," she read aloud. "What do they mean?" "Your skin color," I told her. She stared at me blankly for a few moments. "Who cares?" she asked, genuinely baffled.[5]

This girl's point of view should be every teacher's goal for their multicultural class. Not only do the lessons we learn from Jesus and the Samaritan woman help us connect with our diverse students, it also teaches us how to connect with the adults in our profession—the parents and guardians of our students and our colleagues. Each year when I was assigned a senior seminar course, I would invite second-year alumni who taught in the area to come back to campus and share some experiences from their first year of teaching. I would always ask the same question of our graduates, "What was the most important lesson you learned as a first-year teacher?"

I was often encouraged by the valuable insights our graduates had gained and then passed on to my current class of student teachers. But no response surprised me more than the honest admission and wisdom that came from a young pastor's daughter who was teaching in a low-income and ethnically diverse urban school. She had been raised in a quiet, conservative, rural community but had accepted a position in a high-needs, low-performing elementary school. She replied:

> You would think my answer would be that I learned how to teach poor black first graders how to read, but that wasn't my most important lesson. No, I learned that the teacher who taught in the room next to mine—the one who lived with her boyfriend and worked as a lounge

---

5. Stevens, "We All Benefit," 3.

## Jesus and the Student Who Needed Acceptance

singer on weekends—had some very valuable ideas on how to teach reading.

My graduate had to learn to accept advice from someone whose life experiences were quite the opposite of her own. In order to do this, she had to learn to accept this individual. She had to recognize that an individual who had different personal values still had credible professional wisdom. She had to find common goals between them in order to build a relationship with her. This is not possible if we only see the differences that divide us.

I am often asked by my students why they should teach in a public school if they are so limited in sharing their faith with their students. We spend time reviewing and discussing such articles as Schwartz's "Christians Teaching in the Public Schools: What Are Some Options"[6] to help such students determine whether they believe God is calling them to serve in public or private schools at this time. But I also ask them to consider a different public school mission where they are not so limited, that of friendship evangelism with their colleagues. To do this we must, like my graduate, get past personal differences and find common ground for building relationships. Connecting only with those who share our own personal beliefs not only makes us ineffective for Christ, it also damages the gospel message when we segregate ourselves from those who need to hear it and see it lived out in our schools. We are called to be Christ in every relationship we have in our effort to love our neighbor as ourselves. This command extends to the student whose family lives by a different set of moral guidelines or practices a different religion than ours or our other students'.

As a Christian teacher of future educators, I have been asked how Christians could sensitively and effectively teach children or adolescents whose families' beliefs and practices are contrary to their own.[7] To illustrate this dilemma, I use the analogy of children who come from homes where their parents smoke. Smoking cigarettes, although legal, is a practice that has experienced a cultural

---

6. Schwartz, "Christians Teaching," 293–305.
7. See Lederhouse, "Personal Faith," 13–15.

51

shift since the 1960s. Today it is generally regarded as an unhealthy habit that can be detrimental not only to the adult who smokes, but also to the child who breathes in second hand smoke. Is it possible for teachers who do not smoke or believe in the value of smoking to educate the child of a smoker? Do they value these children less than the children of non-smokers? Do they see their responsibility to educate them as any less important than their duty to other individuals? The answer is obvious: of course they don't. Just as they have an ethical responsibility to focus on the learning needs of these students, Christian teachers recognize their ethical responsibility to educate all learners, regardless of their background. More importantly, it is the child who is often shunned by others, for whatever reason, who most needs an understanding adult to offer protection and advocate on his or her behalf.

Another question I have been asked is how teachers who seek to understand the challenges surrounding their diverse students can still demand a high level of performance from those students. This is a struggle for many novices because it is tempting to confuse showing understanding to a student with excusing him or her from meeting certain expectations. Excusing a student from meeting the same expectations as everyone else has led to the achievement gap we see on a national level. Professional educators earn their salary by carefully differentiating instruction and providing resources so that all students can access the concepts or skills needed to reach a learning goal. Balancing the relational aspects of teaching with learning demands is hard for first-year teachers to negotiate. I require my pre-service teachers to memorize this statement: "I am holding you accountable because I care about you and your future."

As indicated by his encounter with the Samaritan woman, Jesus is the best example of showing empathy toward his students without compromising his requirements for them. In ignoring social customs of the day, Jesus modeled his regard for others to his disciples. My fourth grade teaching colleague not only viewed her diverse students as assets, she also modeled this perception to other students in her class and to her faculty. If we, as Christian professional educators, can get past the barrier of perceived differences ourselves, we can serve as models to other faculty members. Rather than see our English learners as problematic, we can articulate the pride we have in students who are bilingual as an increasingly important asset in our country's future. We can welcome students with special needs in our classes. Our role in making all students feel at home in our classrooms requires more than just acceptance and commitment; it also requires continuous education to learn how to teach our diverse students more effectively by adding new evidence-based strategies to our professional skill set as they are developed. To teach like a disciple, we need to value all learners and equip ourselves to teach them effectively, no matter how similar or different from us they may be.

# 6

# The Challenging Jesus and the Gifted Student

## *John 3:1–21*

THE INTERACTION BETWEEN JESUS and Nicodemus, a member of the Jewish ruling council, contains the most familiar verse in the entire Bible—John 3:16. Although this verse is known by millions of Christians around the globe and non-believers as well, it is important to remember that it was first part of a lesson plan for one individual, a Pharisee who sought out the Master Teacher. As we study this encounter found in John 3:1–21, notice how Jesus' method of instructing Nicodemus is distinct from his encounters with less educated individuals.

This encounter between the two religious teachers is a discussion focusing on what is required to enter the kingdom of God. It is here that Jesus introduces the concept of being "born again" (John 3:3) or being born from above, referring to a spiritual rebirth that releases one from the penalty of sin. Despite his prior knowledge and profession, Nicodemus questioned this concept on both literal and figurative levels, revealing how little he understood the concept. Jesus then disclosed God's plan of salvation to Nicodemus and Christ's own pivotal, sacrificial role in making this spiritual rebirth possible.

## What do we know about Nicodemus?

John's first descriptor of Nicodemus is that he was a member of the Jewish ruling council. Not only was he a Pharisee, he was a high-ranking Pharisee with a seat on the Sanhedrin, the Jewish supreme court.[1] As Bruner describes Nicodemus, "It is difficult to imagine a person more qualified to be a good human being or to enjoy a good relation with God or, at least, to ask the right questions than this Nicodemus."[2] He was educated in the Scriptures, a teacher of the law, and an important decision-maker in his role on the council. Similar in background to the rich young ruler, Nicodemus appears to have had all the makings of a class valedictorian. He had extensive background knowledge, strong reasoning skills, and an inquisitive nature. What more could a teacher want in a student?

The second contextual piece in this passage is the fact that Nicodemus came to Jesus at night. Bruner sees two possible reasons for John to include the time of day in this account. Nicodemus either wanted privacy for an individual conversation with Jesus, or he wanted to avoid criticism from his peers.[3] He either waited so that he could meet with Jesus after the crowds had gone home for the evening or he wanted to avoid a rebuke from fellow Pharisees who were hostile to the Galilean. Either set of circumstances reveals Nicodemus' earnest intent to determine for himself who Jesus was.

We also know that Nicodemus believed Jesus' authority came from God. He respectfully calls him "Rabbi," a term for "teacher" that Nicodemus himself would have been called. He had determined this teacher's divine appointment from the signs or miracles Jesus had performed. Nicodemus may have been witness to these acts himself or heard of them from reputable sources. At this point, his perception of Jesus was based on this physical evidence and Nicodemus' own knowledge of the Scriptures. His statement recorded in the second verse, "We know you are a teacher who has

1. Gundry, *Commentary on the New Testament*, 359.
2. Bruner, *Gospel of John*, 166.
3. Ibid.

come from God," resonated with John in that the apostle begins his gospel with this same message. In the first chapter, John similarly writes that Jesus was sent from God but that he had this authority not merely because God appointed him; rather, this authority came from the fact that he was God himself. This truth required more than Nicodemus' reason or knowledge; it required him to have faith.

We can also infer that Nicodemus was intelligent. He didn't come to Jesus out of grief or in need of healing, as was the case with Mary Magdalene or the woman who touched his garment. Nicodemus came to Jesus, in part, from intellectual curiosity. He wanted to know whether Jesus was merely a teacher or the promised Messiah of the Scriptures. His appearance on Jesus' doorstep reveals his openness to learning. Rather than feeling threatened by Jesus like the other Jewish leaders, Nicodemus wanted to know the truth. He demonstrated intellectual virtue by seeking him out even though doing so carried substantial risk for him.

## What do we know about Jesus from this interaction?

Jesus recognized his student's capability. He understood Nicodemus' rich academic, theological, and experiential background. As a result, he began his lesson by suggesting an impossible task—to be a citizen of God's kingdom in heaven, one had to be born again. Nicodemus first took this directive literally, responding that no one could re-enter their mother's womb to experience another birth.

Jesus, however, was speaking metaphorically, choosing his figurative language carefully. As was true for the rich young ruler, Nicodemus was born into the right circumstances. He was well educated and had achieved an influential position in the Jewish hierarchy. Nicodemus was accomplished and therefore should have qualified to be a kingdom citizen in good standing by reason of his first birth—his upbringing, his education at the synagogue, and his present leadership role. But Jesus' metaphor dispelled this popular premise. None of one's earthly accomplishments has any bearing on whether one is part of the kingdom of God. Jesus spoke of spiritual, not physical, birth—the act of being born from above. This type of birth is part of the unseen world. He likened the mysterious aspect of spiritual rebirth to that of the wind, a force whose effects one could sense without seeing it, knowing how it came to be, or where it would go next.

When Nicodemus questioned this abstract concept, Jesus challenged him further, asking how, as an influential and learned spiritual teacher, he could be so limited in his thinking about spiritual regeneration. Jesus did not cut Nicodemus any slack. He pushed harder in his instructional approach, stating that if Nicodemus could not understand aspects of the physical, natural world—phenomena that he could observe—he could not possibly understand concepts from the spiritual, heavenly realm in order to believe. Jesus' gave no hint of concern for Nicodemus' self-esteem in this dialogue. He was no soft-spoken Sunday school teacher with this capable student; instead, he was a stern and demanding coach.

Christ then made the claim that only one person on earth could speak from personal experience about heaven—the Son of Man. He could claim this because he himself was the only One sent by the Father from heaven to earth. His mission on earth was not only to tell others of the way back to their Heavenly Father; he became that Way. He foretold his own crucifixion to Nicodemus by drawing an analogy between Israel's salvation from looking on the snake Moses had lifted up in the desert and the coming time when he himself would be lifted up on a cross. Undoubtedly familiar with this history of his ancestors, Nicodemus was not given a full explanation of this comparison, but I am sure he reflected on it often after Jesus' death.

I have to confess that for a long time I separated Nicodemus and Christ's conversation about being born again from the section of the chapter that contains John 3:16–21. I am sure there is disagreement among biblical scholars as to whether the words recorded in the John 3:16–21 passage were spoken by Jesus directly to Nicodemus or are the gospel writer's explanation of Jesus' further conversation with Nicodemus. But my NIV Bible and commentator Frederick Dale Bruner[4] indicate these are Jesus' own words. Even if they are John's summary of Jesus' message to Nicodemus, they contain a context specifically applicable to the Sanhedrin council member.

The truths expressed in these six verses use vocabulary familiar to the work of a high court official. Nicodemus served as a judge in religious matters. As a member of the Sanhedrin council, he could convict or exonerate individuals, either freeing them of wrongdoing or turning them over to Roman authorities for trial and punishment. Jesus formatted his entire lesson to connect the content of his identity with this student's background. He used the terms "stands condemned" to describe humanity's position before God due to sin and used "verdict" to describe the amazing reason why we are not condemned: Jesus, the Light of the World, has come into the world not to condemn it but to save it. This salvation, or acquittal, is offered to the entire world—not just the Jews—solely through belief in the saving work of God's one and only Son. Without this belief, every person faces eternal punishment.

Jesus' last statement in John 3:21, "but whoever lives by the truth comes into the light, so that it may be seen plainly that what he has done has been done through God," ties the message of salvation back to his opening statement, "you must be born again." This second birth is due to God's supreme sacrifice, not our own efforts. Jesus may not have offered Nicodemus an "exit slip" to assess whether he grasped the important points of the lesson, but I am sure he gave Nicodemus much to think about, particularly because he set this lesson within a legal framework that Nicodemus could more easily understand.

## What can we learn from Nicodemus?

One of the most wonderful aspects of meeting Nicodemus in this interaction from John's Gospel is that, unlike the account of the rich young ruler, this narrative does give us glimpses of how

---

4. Ibid., 200–209.

Nicodemus ended his spiritual journey. There is evidence that he moved beyond mere reason and knowledge regarding the person of Jesus Christ and came to faith. John references Nicodemus defending Jesus to other Pharisees later in his gospel, stating, "Does our law condemn a man without first hearing him to find out what he has been doing?"(John 7:50–51). Then, in John 19:39–40, we read that Nicodemus accompanied Joseph of Arimathea to prepare and entomb Jesus' body after his crucifixion. I don't believe Nicodemus would have taken the risk of caring for Jesus' body if he had not had a prior close relationship with him.

Unlike the record of the Samaritan woman and the sick woman's encounters with Jesus, there is no indication that Nicodemus became a disciple of Christ the night he first met with him. John does not end this chapter with "and Nicodemus believed that Jesus was the Son of God." More likely, Nicodemus' decision to follow Christ took time. He probably spent a great deal of time contemplating the truths Jesus had revealed to him before making the conscious decision to commit his life to serving him. Nicodemus is an example of one whose faith in Christ is based on intellectual reasoning as well as experience.

Another lesson gained from Nicodemus is that learning only occurs when we are not afraid to reveal what we don't understand. He could have just nodded his head to everything Jesus said without questioning him or asking for clarification. We all know of students who respond this way; they don't ask questions or make any indication that they are not catching on to what we are teaching. I have been this student myself on occasions when I have been confused by what the instructor was saying but failed to interact with him or her because I didn't want to reveal my ignorance. This would have been the easier path for Nicodemus to take, particularly because his ignorance could have caused Jesus to question his qualifications as a religious teacher. And that is exactly what Jesus did; he challenged Nicodemus' authority to teach when he didn't appear to understand fundamental spiritual concepts. Nicodemus was humbled by his own questions, but it appears that he asked them despite this risk because he earnestly wanted to know the truth.

## What can we learn from Jesus in this interaction?

The most essential lesson we learn from Jesus is our theological understanding of redemption. He clearly lays out his mission through his discussion with Nicodemus. God loved us so much that he sent his Son to pay our penalty for sin. None of us can pay this penalty and earn God's forgiveness through our own efforts. Without accepting Jesus' sacrifice, we are condemned, because we fail to acknowledge God's provision of his Son's sacrificial act of redemption.

Jesus' form of pedagogy is tailored to his capable student. He challenged the Pharisee through complex imagery, taking into account his student's familiarity with the Scriptures. But Jesus also described his mission of redemption in language that would be commonplace to a judge. His contextualized description attests to Jesus' care in constructing his lesson for the individual, even when that individual had advanced background knowledge.

We also see that while Jesus pressed Nicodemus to consider spiritual matters on a deeper level, he did not press him to act on the truths he heard that evening. He extended no "altar call." As was true for C. S. Lewis,[5] it may have taken some time for the truth to win out over Nicodemus' reasons for resisting the gospel.

We don't all come to Christ on the same timetable. In his 1954 autobiography, Lewis writes that God pursues us much more intensely than we ever seek him, going so far as to describe the period of his life before conversion as "God's assault."[6] Ultimately, it is our choice to surrender our resistance and accept God's gift of salvation. Offering us this choice is characteristic of our relational God. He wants to enter into a relationship that we desire to have

---

5. See Lewis, *Surprised by Joy.*
6. Ibid., 266.

## The Challenging Jesus and the Gifted Student

with him, and he is as patient with us as he was with Nicodemus in waiting for our surrender.

## What can we, as educators, learn from this interaction?

One of the educational applications drawn from the chapter on the rich young ruler focused on the need to make content accessible to all students—including students eligible for special education services and English learners—but to then hold students accountable for their effort in meeting the academic goal. The focus on learning expectations in the chapter on the Samaritan woman included the need for teachers to maintain high expectations for students whose backgrounds are different from their own. Teachers must also hold their very capable students to appropriate standards. One might think that these students would have no difficulty meeting standards-based expectations. This would be true if knowledge and performance expectations are designed for the average learner and then applied to all students, but strong teachers know to raise the bar for their advanced learners.

Each time I have taught an introductory course on exceptional children and adolescents, I have asked my students why we need to provide a rigorous alternative form of education for intellectually gifted students. I have often heard such responses as the need for our country to keep its competitive edge or the need to help all children, who are created in God's image, achieve their full potential. These are both valid responses to the question, but I have seldom heard the one I see as most important: the need for gifted students to experience struggle and failure. Without such an intervention, gifted students are the group that actually learns the least from a middle or high school course or year in elementary school because they generally enter each classroom with the most prior knowledge.[7] Spending the year or semester reviewing information they already know is not inviting and results in these

---

7. Winebrenner, *Teaching Gifted Kids*, 1.

students failing to deepen their conceptual understanding. As a result, too many gifted learners disengage from the educational system altogether.

For those highly capable students who remain invested, learning in a typical academic environment comes so easily that they often fail to learn resiliency—the ability to survive hardship and disappointment—which is an important life skill. All students need to develop resiliency, but gifted students can find themselves the least equipped to cope with the significant difficulties life brings because they have so seldom experienced academic failure. We need to challenge them at an appropriate level by differentiating the curriculum. This is most frequently done by compacting,[8] accelerating,[9] or enriching it through project-based learning.[10] We need to give these students choices so that they can pursue the required content at a level appropriate to their capabilities.

One of the most valuable definitions of teaching I encountered in the course of my career was from early childhood educator Judith Collier. She shared in a professional development session that teaching could be defined as extending an invitation to participate. As educators, we cannot make students learn; we can only invite them to participate in learning. Sometimes we only need to extend one invitation, but most often we have to issue several invitations before all of our students will join us in the learning process.

Students can be reluctant to participate for several reasons. Sometimes they don't feel capable of participating; the content seems too remote from their experience, too difficult, or too irrelevant. Such students don't believe they have the skill set to participate; they perceive the requirements to be beyond their capability. Others may find the invitation unappealing. The content is already familiar to them or the task is not rigorous enough to engage them.

In the former case, the teacher needs to supply enough background knowledge to connect the student's world to the content and to ensure that the student has the prerequisite skills to

8. Ibid., 179–80.
9. Ibid., 191–98.
10. Ibid., 85.

accomplish the independent portion of the learning task. In the latter case, the students need rigor; learning expectations need to be higher. The teacher needs to allow choice in both the aspects of the content and the assessment format so that the student can develop a depth of understanding beyond the student's current grasp of the concept. Optional forms of assessment allow gifted students to be creative in demonstrating this newfound understanding.

At other times, students may be unable to participate fully because of the time constraints in which teachers and students must operate. The clock is the greatest enemy of the school day or instructional period. It works against teaching and learning activities that require sustained, high-level thinking in order to develop a depth of conceptual understanding. It often breaks learning activities into such short segments that students can only achieve surface knowledge. While a spiral curriculum is designed to recover a concept or topic at a later point in time, the length of the exposure and the time period between exposures are often inappropriate for some students.

On a more positive note, we are currently in a period where educational research has demonstrated that less is more.[11] Many of our curriculum standards, such as the Common Core State Standards in Mathematics, have been revised to cover less content material but in greater depth, focusing on applying key principles and concepts over the memorization of facts.[12] This affords students the necessary time to understand critical content through analysis, synthesis, and critique.

As evidenced throughout the New Testament, one does not have to be an intellectual to receive Christ's gift of salvation. But this is not to say that faith is incompatible with reason. Some of the greatest creative and intellectual minds, such as those of Lewis,[13]

11. See Dweck, *Mindset*, 193–202; Furner and Robinson, "Using TIMSS," 3; Schmidt, "Seizing the Moment for Mathematics," 24–25.

12. See Wiggins and McTighe, *Understanding by Design*, 126–45; National Governors Association Center for Best Practices and the Council of Chief State School Officers, *Common Core State Standards*; and NGSS Lead States, *Next Generation Science Standards*.

13. See Bonhoeffer, *Cost of Discipleship*.

Kierkegaard, [14] and Bonhoeffer,[15] have come to Christ through thoughtful engagement with theological principles. In teaching his capable student, Nicodemus, Jesus recognized the importance of addressing the mind as well as the heart. He modeled this by confronting Nicodemus' own reasoning and then explaining his content in a framework familiar to his bright student. Jesus was unafraid to push him by capitalizing on his intellectual abilities to understand. To teach like a disciple, we must challenge our students to think.

14. See Kierkegaard, *Works of Love*.
15. See Lewis, *Mere Christianity*.

7

# The Patient Jesus and the Student Who Craved Attention

## Matt 14:22-33; Matt 16:13-19; Matt 26:31-35, 69-75; John 21: 15-23

I BELIEVE THAT IF the Apostle Peter had been enrolled in my third grade class, he would undoubtedly be the boy in the front row wildly waving his raised arm and yelling, "Pick me! Pick me!" to every question I posed. This behavior would be followed by an audible sigh of disappointment whenever he would not be called on to respond. Or in a middle school, he would be the socially awkward student who typically blurts out an answer before hearing the complete question, often embarrassing himself at the moment, though never enough to change the habit. Can't you just picture these two scenarios?

We have all had these students in our classes, experiencing them either when we were learners or as teachers. Perhaps you were a Peter in the classroom yourself. I have often thought I would love to have heard Peter preach, but I doubt I would have found it easy to have him on my class roster. How do we help students like Peter who exhibit a strong need for attention? How did Jesus respond to Peter's impulsiveness and need to be noticed?

### What do we know about Peter?

Peter and his brother, Andrew, were the first two of the twelve apostles to be called by Jesus (Matt 4:18). They were both fishermen in Galilee. We don't know whether they had an exceptionally good or poor catch that morning, but we are told they immediately left their nets and followed Christ. We have evidence that Peter was married because Matt 8:14–17 describes the account of Jesus healing Peter's mother-in-law.

When he was first called, Peter's name was Simon. Although it has been translated as "pebble" or small stone, Simon was also a Hebrew name meaning "God has heard." But at one point in his ministry, Jesus changed Simon's name to Peter. In Matt 16:13–19, Jesus first asked his disciples what others were saying about him. After listening to their various responses, he next asked them who *they* believed him to be. Simon immediately declared to Jesus, "You are the Christ, the Son of the living God." In response, Jesus proclaimed:

> Blessed are you, Simon son of Jonah, for this was not revealed to you by flesh and blood, but by my Father in heaven. And I tell you that you are Peter, and on this rock I will build my church, and the gates of death will not overcome it. (Matt 16:17–18)

The Greek name "Petros," or Peter, means "rock." This is the same root found in "petroleum" and "petrified." Renaming Peter as a rock conveyed strength and resilience. Peter now had a demanding name to embody.

However, this apostle and eventual leader of the church had several weaknesses. Throughout the gospels we see Peter's need for affirmation. In the account of the rich young ruler, we read of Peter reminding Jesus that although the ruler could not give up his wealth, he and the other disciples had left everything to follow him (Mark 10:17–31). Simon Peter seemed to be begging for some word of praise from Jesus for his sacrifice.

This need for attention also made Peter appear to be a bit competitive. He seemed to be interested in everyone else's business in order to see how he ranked in comparison with others. Even when Jesus forgave and restored Peter for denying him, Peter wanted to know how John's future would compare with his own

(John 21:21–22). His insecurities surfaced even at this late point in his relationship with Jesus.

We also see Peter's impulsivity. In several interactions, we can see him acting first and reflecting later. When the apostles saw a ghostlike figure walking on the surface of rough waters, Jesus identified himself and told them not to be afraid. Upon learning that it was his teacher, Peter asked if he could join him. He jumped out of the boat without any hesitation or knowledge of what to do. Soon he began to sink and needed Jesus to rescue him (Matt 14:22–33).

Peter also spoke when he didn't know what else to do. At the transfiguration, Peter, James, and John witnessed Jesus conversing with Moses and Elijah. Luke indicates that Peter was at a loss for words and so blurted out that they should erect a shelter for all three great men (Luke 9:33). Instead of remaining silent like the other two disciples, Peter felt the need to make a comment. More than likely, all of us have stood in Peter's awkward position of saying something without thinking and then regretting it afterward.

Although Peter's intentions may have been pure, he still spoke and acted inappropriately. Right after proclaiming that Jesus was the Christ, the Son of God, Peter refuted Jesus' prophesy that he must suffer and die (Matt 16:21–23). Jesus rebuked him for denying the truth of this statement, even calling him "Satan" in his reproach. In Gethsemane, Jesus had to correct Peter again, this time for recklessly taking a sword and maiming a member of the group sent to arrest him (John 18:10–11).

Occasionally, Peter's impulsivity surfaced in his inability to follow directions without requiring special attention. In John 13 we read that Jesus modeled servanthood by washing the feet of his disciples at the Last Supper. At first, Peter adamantly refused to have Jesus wash his feet, but after being told by Jesus that he must obey, Peter then wanted Jesus to wash his hands and head as well. Jesus had to remind Peter that he needed to do what he was asked to do in order to receive the same treatment as his fellow disciples. Later at that same event, Peter sought to elevate his own position by making the grandiose claim that even if all the other disciples abandoned Christ, he would never fall away (Matt 26:33). Jesus then warned Peter that he would disown him no less than three times that very same night.

Although the four gospel writers identify more character flaws in Peter than any other disciple, they also describe his strengths. He was incredibly courageous. No one else ventured out of the boat when Jesus approached them in rough seas. Despite his inability to live up to his pledge, no other disciple promised to be loyal to Christ with as much conviction as Peter did. John records Peter's response to Jesus' question of whether the twelve disciples would abandon him like others had: "Lord, to whom should we go? You have the words of eternal life. We have come to believe and to know that you are the Holy One of God" (John 6:67–69).

Knowing that he might face death himself, Peter still defended Jesus in the garden of Gethsemane by wielding a sword. His devotion was unmatched, even if it was misguided or unproven at times. His need for recognition was based on the truth that he had indeed sacrificed much to follow Christ. His refusal to accept the truth that Jesus must suffer and die was based solely on his deep love for his teacher.

Peter may have been insecure about his own competency, but he had great confidence in his decision to follow Christ. He unreservedly believed Jesus was the Messiah he claimed to be. Given his courage, his loyalty, and his conviction, it is no surprise that Peter was the apostle chosen to give the sermon recorded in Acts 2:14–36, which "pulled no punches" in identifying who Jesus was and proclaiming that Israel needed to seek forgiveness for having rejected him. Because of Peter's strengths, it is also no surprise that Jesus chose him to lead his church.

Peter's great influence extends even to the church today through the Gospel of Mark. Mark was an associate of Peter and is believed to have written down Peter's teachings on the life of Jesus. Many scholars believed this took place in Italy, probably after Peter was martyred.[1]

---

1. Witherington, *Gospel of Mark*, 21–22.

# The Patient Jesus and the Student Who Craved Attention

## What do we know about Jesus from this interaction?

Unlike passages we have previously studied to learn about Jesus' relationships with his students, his interaction with Peter is not confined to one occasion but is instead found throughout the four gospel accounts. Even our focus here on several specific interactions between Jesus and Peter is by no means complete. However, we do see a pattern of response from the teacher across all these events.

When the rich young ruler was unable to comply with the demand to give away his wealth and therefore left dejected, Jesus commented on how hard it was for the rich to enter the kingdom of God (Mark 10:24). Peter focused attention back on himself by reminding Jesus that they, the disciples, had left everything to follow him. Instead of giving sympathy or a compliment, Jesus assured Peter that *anyone* who made sacrifices to follow him would receive a hundred times more blessings in this life as well as eternal life in the next. There was no feeding of Peter's ego here.

In Matt 14:22-33, we read the account of Jesus approaching the disciples by walking on water. When Peter asked Jesus to invite him to join him on the surface of the waves, Jesus told him to come. Peter leaped out of the boat but soon became concerned about the wind and started sinking. When Peter cried out to Jesus to save him, Jesus reached out and caught him, admonishing him for his doubt. Again, there are no recorded compliments for Peter on his bravery.

Jesus rescued Peter again in the garden of Gethsemane when, in an attempt to defend Jesus, Peter had grabbed a sword and sliced off the ear of Malchus, the high priest's servant (John 18:10-11). Despite how well-intentioned Peter's action may have been, Jesus extended no thank-you to Peter but instead healed the servant's ear and commanded Peter to put the sword away, informing him that he must drink the cup of suffering and death that his Father had given him. This was not the first time Jesus had to correct Peter for interfering with Jesus' mission. Earlier in his ministry, Jesus rebuked Peter when he refused to accept Jesus' prophetic word regarding his suffering and death (Matt 16:21-23). He had referred to Peter as "Satan" and "a stumbling block" because Peter responded from a human perspective rather than seeing the Father's ultimate assignment for his Son.

Peter's competitive edge, which accompanied his need for special recognition, was present throughout the Last Supper. Each time it surfaced, Jesus corrected him. When Peter first refused to have his feet washed, Jesus told him to obey like the others. When he then wanted Jesus to wash his hands and head too, Jesus again reminded him to obey as the others had. It seems that Peter had a hard time being treated no differently than his peers.

Later that evening, Peter assured Jesus that even if his fellow disciples turned away, he would lay down his life for him. Jesus offered no gratitude for this pledge but instead responded:

> Simon, Simon, Satan has asked to sift you as wheat. But I have prayed for you, Simon, that your faith may not fail. And when you have turned back, strengthen your brothers... I tell you, Peter, before the rooster crows today, you will deny three times that you know me. (Luke 22:31-32, 34)

Jesus did not soften the blow when forewarning Peter of his upcoming failure, but he did show his love for Peter by intervening for him so that his faith would protect him from Satan's grasp. Implicit in this decree was Jesus' lesson to Peter to remember this failure so that he would be able to show understanding and offer encouragement when his fellow apostles similarly wavered in their commitment. The scar from this wound would remind Peter of his own weakness and, in turn, help him become a more humble leader.

Finally, when Peter had turned back, his competitiveness was still evident even after Jesus had forgiven and reinstated him for denying him three times. In John 21:15-23, we read that Jesus asked Peter an equal number of times whether he loved him. I call this passage one of the first performance assessments recorded in history because each time Peter assured Jesus that he loved him, Jesus gave him an assignment to perform. Peter was a man of action, so Jesus gave him three leadership tasks: feed his lambs, take care of his sheep, and feed his sheep. Jesus then soberly foretold Peter's own martyrdom by stating that one day he would be led where he did not want to go. Upon seeing John nearby, Peter quickly asked what would happen to him. Jesus reminded him that it really was none of his business: "If I want him to remain alive until I return, what is that to you?" (John 21:21). Even at this point, Jesus was still coaching Peter to keep his focus on the things that matter.

## What can we learn from Peter?

Given that Peter knew how his own betrayal of Jesus had come just hours after he had promised him his loyalty, I have often wondered why Peter did not take his life like Judas did. I doubt that when Judas agreed to turn Jesus over to members of the Sanhedrin he was aware of how tragically this action in Gethsemane would play out over the next twenty-four hours. He likely did not anticipate that Jesus' arrest would ultimately lead to his death by crucifixion. Judas' realization that his plan had gone horribly wrong and that his action made him complicit in Jesus' execution prompted him to hang himself. Most likely, Judas did not foresee his role's dreadful result.

However, Peter was fully aware that he would deny being a follower of Jesus. He had heard directly from Jesus' own lips that he would go back on his word and disavow any knowledge or relationship with Christ. And he had not only heard the nature of this denial, he had also heard the frequency and timing of it.

Unlike Judas, Peter had a very close relationship with Jesus. Because disappointing those we hold close typically affects us more deeply than failing those we know from a distance, Peter was probably as remorseful over his personal failure as Judas was. We read in Matt 26:75 that when he heard the rooster crow, Peter remembered Jesus' words and wept bitterly. His act of cowardice when Jesus most needed him must have haunted him throughout his life, yet Peter was able to move past his failure, while Judas could not. Why did the outcomes differ so greatly between these two men?

I believe there are several reasons for Peter's choosing life over death in the wake of extreme failure. First, this was not the only time Peter had done the wrong thing. As indicated earlier, Peter had a history of saying or doing the wrong thing. I do not think it was coincidence that it was Peter who asked Jesus in Matt 18:21–35 how many times he was expected to forgive someone. I think forgiveness was on Peter's mind quite a bit because of his impulsive nature. He himself had experienced Jesus' forgiveness time and time again.

But it was not just this pattern of forgiveness that affected Peter. It was also Peter's belief in the power of Jesus' forgiveness. This belief was grounded in his close relationship with the Savior. He had heard Jesus forgive sins when he healed a paralyzed man dropped through a Capernaum ceiling (Mark 2:1–12). He had heard Jesus forgive the sins of the adulterous woman (John 8:1–11). Many times, he had witnessed the healing power of Jesus' forgiveness in others in addition to experiencing it himself.

Peter had a close relationship with the One who offered forgiveness. Unlike Judas, Peter was part of Jesus' inner circle. He was at the transfiguration with John and James (Luke 9:28). As a member of this same trio, he accompanied Jesus into Jairus' home and watched as Jesus brought the man's daughter back to life (Mark 5:37). The three disciples also walked with Jesus to Gethsemane before his arrest (Matt 26:37). His relationship with Jesus was as "up close and personal" as one could get. From that relationship he had learned two truths: Jesus was exactly who he claimed to be—the Son of God—and, equally important, Jesus loved him. Judas died in despair without hope of restoration for what he had done, but Peter lived with the hope that Jesus, his loving Savior, would forgive him again.

# The Patient Jesus and the Student Who Craved Attention

## What can we learn from Jesus in this interaction?

Jesus was an amazing model of patience as he helped Peter move his focus off himself and onto his mission. When Simon Peter met Jesus, he was filled with insecurities that were demonstrated in competitiveness, impulsivity, and other attention-getting behaviors. It is hard to recognize this Peter as the same one who delivered the Pentecostal sermon that added 3,000 members to the church in one day. However, this transformation took time. It involved continuous correction and redirection from a mentor who recognized that Peter was worth this investment.

As a teacher, Jesus had a remarkable ability to see students as a balance of strengths and weaknesses. While he didn't ignore their vulnerabilities, he didn't let his students' faults cloud his perception of their potential. Yes, Peter was impulsive, but he had great courage. He was reckless at times, but this recklessness grew into boldness for the gospel. He was impetuous but fearless. With instruction, Jesus recognized that Peter would make a resilient leader.

Being the Great Teacher, Jesus wholly accepted Peter as he was, but he didn't let Peter's limitations go unchecked. When Peter craved attention, Jesus redirected him to more important truths. When he acted impulsively, Jesus corrected him. Jesus not only reformed Peter's bad habits; he developed the apostle's strengths into the qualities of a great leader. He mentored unreflective Peter into a mature apostle, transforming Peter's self-focus to a kingdom focus.

I have stood in Rome near the sites where Peter is said to have been imprisoned, crucified, and entombed. Whether or not these locations are accurate is secondary to the realization that this impulsive, insecure fisherman became a powerful guardian of the gospel, defender of the Christian faith, and martyr for the kingdom of God. All of this took place because a teacher saw great promise in a student who craved attention.

## What can we, as educators, learn from this interaction?

When we feel stressed or anxious about people or events that matter to us, we all tend to exhibit signs of impulsivity, competitiveness, or attention-seeking behavior. As a primary grade teacher, I soon came to recognize changes in behavior that indicated when one of my children in kindergarten or first grade had just acquired a new sibling. Often, the temporary decrease in attention at home resulted in an increased need for attention at school, particularly if the student had been an only child before the baby's arrival. None of the children who exhibited this need was even aware of its cause. Displays of attention-getting behavior like this are most often due to feeling insecure. It is my experience that when children or adults fear a lack of acceptance, they feel a need to prove their worth to others. They do this by drawing attention to themselves either positively or negatively.

However, when one of our students continually displays these social and emotional behaviors at an extreme level even under normal circumstances, it may indicate a need for intervention from specialists. As educators, we must be alert to signs of severe problems and initiate the process that will enable these students to receive the type of help they need and deserve. But students like Peter do not fall into this category. Their behavior, while at times disruptive, does not typically interfere with their ability or their classmates' ability to learn. And, as with Peter, we don't always find out the cause of this attention-seeking behavior, but this doesn't imply that we should not address it.

One of the great limitations of classroom teaching is that we typically serve our students in groups. Our profession does not offer the luxury of being able to see our clients one at a time as those in the profession of medicine or law can. When I hear that teachers have an easy job just working from the end of August to June, I often tease back that when physicians and attorneys are required to diagnose illnesses or try cases in groups of no less than twenty-five, then they will start asking for their summers off too. But in all seriousness, our effectiveness at running our practice falls under the category of "classroom management." This concept focuses on how well we can facilitate the process by which our children and adolescents learn to function as members of a group, not just as individuals. Books on classroom management are generally written to provide educators with strategies that enable students to modify their individual behavior sufficiently for group learning.

Think of how differently we could practice our profession and how well we could come to know our students, if we could just hold one-on-one conversations with them every day—if we could serve more as tutors than as teachers. Even Jesus did not have the lengthy class rosters that some of today's teachers have. Developing a mentoring relationship with one of twelve students is far different than teaching one of perhaps 150 students and seeing each group of thirty for less than an hour every day. Middle and high school teachers do not have nearly enough space in their schedule to reach out to every student who displays the needs Peter did in the same way that Jesus was able to interact with him.

The challenge in working with a large group is finding the time to get to know our students as individuals in order to make them feel valued and secure. To be effective teachers, we cannot assume we already know enough about our students to teach them well. We need to uncover our students' interpersonal strengths and general interests as well as their academic and social weaknesses. Weaknesses loom large for us as educators because they usually create a challenge to group learning. Unfortunately, external pressures generally focus on group achievement to the extent that if we are not careful, we can start to see students first in terms of problems their differences create rather than the rich potential they hold for our learning community. For example, do we see a gifted child who happens to have a learning disability, or do we only see their need for accommodations in two separate special education categories? Jesus had a realistic perspective of Peter, but he didn't let Peter's weaknesses distort his vision of Peter's potential for growth. If Jesus had, he never would have invested so much time in mentoring him.

The key to helping students who crave attention is getting past our assumptions about their behaviors in order to find out what they truly think, know, and aspire to become. Literacy professor Steven Layne reminds us that the four most important words for teachers to say are "I thought of you" when used in the context of offering students specifically chosen learning materials that reflect their individual personalities and interests.[2] But to know what materials would engage an individual student, we need to take the time and create the structures for gathering this information. Interest inventories and small group discussion activities provide us with opportunities in the classroom to genuinely get to know what our individual students have experienced and what they value. Casual conversations over lunch, greeting students at the door, and talking with students at extracurricular events are ways we can offer personal attention outside of the classroom.[3] Insights gained from these interactions, in turn, enable us to show that we value our students as socially complex human beings. When students feel valued and secure, they tend to decrease their attention-getting behaviors.

One veteran kindergarten teacher would never pass up an opportunity to mentor a student teacher not only as a chance to share her expertise with a novice, but also to create a structure for extended one-on-one time with each of her children. During the weeks when her student teacher held full responsibility for instruction, this expert teacher would spend each morning and afternoon with a different student at the back of the room. They would converse, read together, and play math games. Although she also used this time as an opportunity to individually assess oral language development, literacy, and numeracy, she most valued it for gaining a better understanding of each child. The more interaction she had with these students, the more secure they felt in this critical first year of school.

When I asked a veteran Chicago public school teacher how she was surviving her class of thirty-seven third grade students that

---

2 Layne, *Igniting a Passion,* 15.

3. Marzano, Marzano, and Pickering, *Classroom Management,* 53.

year, her answer was "Divide and conquer." She said she scheduled at least two volunteers or education students to work in the room with her each period so that she could maintain a 1:12 ratio. She found that any larger number did not allow her to know her students well enough to instruct them effectively. On some days, I observed five adults in the room leading guided reading or math talks with no more than seven children in each group. Because she met their individual needs so effectively this way, her large class of eight- and nine-year-olds was on task more often than any class of older students I observed at the school that semester.

As a professor of education, I realize that maturing as a teacher takes time. Teacher candidates that seem scattered in the college classroom may need the context of an elementary, middle, or high school classroom to pull it all together. Knowing this from experience, I need to be alert to signs of potential in addition to actualized skills. Conversely, sometimes the perfectionist teacher candidate—the one who always has her lesson plans perfectly polished and turned in ahead of schedule—doesn't survive the curveballs of actual practice, while the teacher I see as being too laid-back in my course ultimately has the flexibility to deal with those curveballs and ends up hitting a lot of home runs throughout her teaching career. We have all had students who surprised us in this way. Like Jesus, we need to see students' traits for their potential advantages as well as any possible detrimental effects.

Although he was patient, we don't see much evidence of Jesus affirming Peter in the gospel accounts. Nearly all of his recorded responses to Peter's outbursts involve correction or redirection. But we must also remember that Peter was an adult, not a child or an adolescent. While there are many characteristics of Jesus' methods with Peter that we can adapt to our elementary or secondary context, we must be mindful that we work with individuals who are still in their developmental years and, as such, do not have a say in many of the choices that have been made for them. Some of their attention-seeking behaviors that appear in the classroom or on the playground may be coping mechanisms for dealing with issues in their personal lives that are beyond their control.

While we need to show acceptance of our students regardless of their level of social or emotional stability, this does not imply that we ignore poor interpersonal habits. If we are committed to teaching the whole student, we must help these individuals overcome behaviors that keep them from connecting with others and developing friendships. No matter what subject we teach, our goal should be to help our students develop appropriate social skills. This is ultimately important for both their personal and professional lives.

From Jesus' interaction with Peter, we have seen that caring for students who crave attention requires both patience and correction. This correction helps them see and enjoy a world much bigger than their own insecurities. To teach like a disciple, we must encourage our students to move past themselves and focus on others.

8

# The Perceptive Jesus and the Quiet Student

*John 1:1–5, 13:21–30, 20:30–31, 21:24–25;*
*1 John 1:5–10, Rev 1:9–19*

UNLIKE PETER, THE APOSTLE John is not known for many direct comments addressed to Jesus. We have no record of lengthy verbal interactions between the teacher and this disciple. Although John's spoken words are recorded very few times in the gospels (Mark 10:35–37, Luke 9:54, John 13:25), many scholars consider him to be the author of the most widely read gospel, three letters to the early church, and the book of Revelation. But it is not only the volume of writing from this quiet student that is so noteworthy; his imagery is remarkable for an uneducated laborer. Equally significant is his insightful perspective, which reflected a close relationship with his teacher.

## What do we know about John?

We first meet John when Jesus calls him to be a disciple along with his brother, James, not long after he called Simon Peter and Andrew. Like the first two apostles, John and James were both fishermen in business with their father, Zebedee. The gospels also refer to John's mother, Salome, since it is recorded in Matt 20:20–21 that she asked Jesus to give her two sons a place of honor in his kingdom. Mark indicates that it was the two men themselves who requested this position. Regardless of who made the request, we know from this reference that the two brothers had both parents living at the time of Jesus' ministry.

Jesus did not assure John's mother that he would grant her request but instead used it as an opportunity to predict his own suffering and death. He did, however, honor James and John by including them, along with Peter, in his inner circle. These three men were the disciples closest to Jesus. They were the only ones he took with him into Jairus' home when he brought the synagogue leader's daughter back to life (Mark 5:37), allowed them to witness his transfiguration on the mountain with Moses and Elijah (Matt 17:1–9, Mark 9:2–9, Luke 9:28–36), and asked to accompany him to Gethsemane prior to his arrest and trial (Mark 14:33).

Not only is there no account of extensive dialogue between Jesus and John in his Gospel, we have no record of any significant interactions between the Savior and this fisherman in the Synoptic Gospels either. Therefore, the absence of such conversation in John's Gospel is not merely due to modesty on his part. Unlike Peter, John does not appear to stand out in a crowd; he does not get much notice in the gospel accounts, and despite being mentioned at every pivotal point of Christ's ministry, he was not the primary actor on any of these occasions.

However, this lack of time in the spotlight does not indicate that John was timid. Luke records that when John and his brother were in a Samaritan town that did not welcome Jesus, they asked him if they should call down fire from heaven to destroy it (Luke 9:54). Jesus stopped them, however, and had them go to another village. Apparently John was not afraid of confrontation when provoked. This action earned John and his brother the nickname "sons of thunder."

John is the only disciple mentioned as present at the crucifixion, which meant risking everything by remaining near Jesus until he died. John's presence at the cross illustrates his character. This quiet but courageous disciple was loyal to Jesus even when others may have deserted him.

Finally, we also know that John referred to himself throughout his gospel as the disciple Jesus loved or as the "beloved disciple."

On four occasions, John uses this title to describe himself (John 13:23, 19:26, 21:7, 21:20). Note that he does not say he is the disciple Jesus loved *best* but rather the disciple Jesus loved. Because we know that Jesus certainly loved his other disciples, John appears to use this title out of a sense of humility rather than arrogance. He speaks of God's amazing love in 1 John 3:1, "How great is the love the Father has lavished on us, that we should be called children of God!" He then references Jesus' role in this love story in the sixteenth verse of this same chapter, "This is how we know what love is: Jesus Christ laid down his life for us." As an eyewitness to this event who understood the enormity of this action, the disciple chose to identify himself solely as a recipient of this incredible love.

There is a great deal more that biblical scholars have researched about the Apostle John, especially concerning his life after Jesus ascended into heaven, but our focus here is on the relationship he had with his teacher and how that interaction laid the foundation for John's role in proclaiming the gospel after Pentecost. I am continually amazed that the one whose prior work focused on physical strength and manual labor wrote so prolifically and with such figurative language.

## What do we know about Jesus from this interaction?

Since we know that John was not the most extroverted of the apostles, Jesus may have had to initiate much of the interaction between them. According to the evidence we find in the gospels, John was not one to stand out in the group through his actions, questions, or analysis like Peter. Yet he and Jesus were quite close; perhaps he was the closest to Jesus of all the twelve apostles.

First, we know that Jesus selected him to be one of the three in his inner circle of disciples. While James, John, and Peter were among the first apostles Jesus called, being the first members of the twelve apostles could not be the criteria for inclusion, otherwise Andrew, Peter's brother, would have also been a part of this group. Other requirements must have been essential for selection. There was some quality Jesus saw in James, Peter, and John that caused him to invest in their relationships more fully.

Second, we have evidence that John was close to Jesus from a conversation between Peter and John when Jesus announced in the upper room that one of the twelve would betray him (John 13:24–25). After hearing this announcement, all the disciples began to ask each other which one of them it could be. John identifies himself in this passage as the disciple who was sitting right next to the Teacher, actually in a place of honor. Peter then motioned to John to ask Jesus to identify which one of them would do this. Bruner thinks it is noteworthy that Peter went through John to get this information.[1] John, in turn, relayed Peter's question and asked, "Lord, who is it?" Even Peter recognized that John was close to Jesus.

However, as he often did with Peter, Jesus was not hesitant to correct John when he was wrong. The teacher quickly defused John and his brother's misguided plan to call down fire from heaven on those Samaritans who had rejected them. We read in Luke 9:54 that Jesus admonished the "sons of thunder," and they went on to another village.

Third, we know that John and Jesus were close because John attended his crucifixion. Although other disciples may have been present, he is the only one specifically reported to have been there. From the cross, Jesus asked John to provide for his mother. In addition to being responsible, John must have had a generous and compassionate nature in order for Jesus to entrust the care of his heartbroken mother to him.

## What can we learn from John?

One of the most remarkable metaphors used by John to describe Jesus and his impact on the world is the contrast between light and darkness. Jesus referred to himself as "the Light of the World" (John 8:12) and indicated that his followers were to be salt and

---

1. Bruner, *Gospel of John*, 779.

light in terms of doing good and pointing others to God (Matt 5:14), but John uses this term in the opening chapter of his Gospel (John 1:4–9) to indicate Jesus' authority and mission. He also used this contrast in his Gospel (John 3:19–21) to describe the process of redemption, and he drew upon it again in his first letter (1 John 1:5) to encourage fellow believers to be obedient to the truth.

John's contrast between light and darkness in his writing was no doubt far more powerful in his day than ours. I grew up in the city of Chicago, a place where it is never completely dark outside due to the sodium vapor lights that line the city's streets and alleys. They give off a pink cast no matter what hour of the evening or early morning. Growing up, the only time I ever needed to use a flashlight was when my family went to our summer cottage in Wisconsin, since we never experienced total darkness in the city. For years, I couldn't see many winter constellations because it was never dark enough to find any but the brightest stars in my city neighborhood. It took a trip to northern Wisconsin for me to realize the vastness and brilliance of the sky on a clear winter's night.

John, however, lived in an era before electric or gas lighting. As a fisherman, he knew what it was like to be out on a moonless, cloudy night. He understood how total darkness could hide individuals and their actions and just how dangerous it could be on the sea. He also knew the shocking difference a small fire made in the pitch-black early morning hours. This was the context he described to others who heard his message, a context they also knew well. This was the metaphor he chose to illustrate the impact of the sinless, divine Jesus on a fallen world.

John's ability to use imagery made him the best candidate to write the book of Revelation. This portrait of the future required talent in this area in order to depict celestial sights and objects that had no equivalent linguistic expression on earth in either John's time or in ours today. As recorded in Rev 1:19, John was charged personally by the glorified and victorious Jesus to write of what he had seen take place and what was yet to come.

## What can we learn from Jesus in this interaction?

As evidenced by his selection of both Peter and John, we can see that Jesus did not surround himself with students who were clones of one another. He also did not choose the most scholarly individuals as his disciples; the Jewish ruling council identified them as "unschooled and ordinary men" (Acts 4:13). Yet Jesus selected a class of twelve students with diverse personalities and strengths. These students included outspoken Peter and quiet John, several fishermen and a tax collector, one known for doubting him, and even one famous for betraying him. As an educator, Jesus would fail with his student Judas, but he chose him all the same. Jesus did not hand-pick the perfect class in any way.

Tradition and historical texts hold that all Jesus' disciples except John met an untimely and gruesome death as martyrs. While this may seem to be another sign of failure, the fact that each of them gave their lives for Christ's cause demonstrates the strength of their belief in him and the power of his impact and teaching on their lives. The legacy of these men, who varied so greatly from each another, is found in the faith of every worshipping congregation throughout the world today. The evangelizing and discipling ministry of these twelve men, each commissioned by Jesus, has been passed down from generation to generation.

Just like Jesus, none of us will work with a perfect group of people. And probably none of us will work with a group of individuals who are so similar that they are easy to lead. During my experience as a college professor, I agreed in my third year of working on a standing committee to serve as its chair. Unfortunately, I gave my consent before the faculty selected the committee's newest members, who together would comprise one-third of our group. When I saw who had won the election, I strongly questioned my decision. Two of the three individuals were extreme opposites in their disciplinary background, temperament, experience, and opinion. My first thought was "How can I get these two individuals to agree on anything?" I felt overwhelmed. But I soon realized that I was asking the wrong question; I probably couldn't get the two committee members to agree on any issue. Instead, I should have asked myself, "How can I get these two very different people to keep focused on our mission?" That I could do, and as I did, I came to understand how valuable both of these individuals were to our committee's process. Their diverse perspectives were integral to the decisions we needed to make. I found myself believing and reminding my committee that if our nine-member team always viewed issues from the same vantage point, eight of us would be unnecessary. As a result of our diversity, we held rich discussions before making well-reasoned decisions.

Peter and John may not have been similar in either personality or in their relationship to Jesus. Peter may have felt some competitiveness toward John, as we see at Peter's restoration. John might have even rolled his eyes on occasion when Peter asked yet another question of Jesus. But the two certainly overcame their differences after Jesus' time on earth through their courageous commitment to their Savior and Lord. In chapters 3 and 4 of Acts, we see how these two very different apostles worked together to preach the gospel and heal the sick. They were even imprisoned together and tried by the Sanhedrin for preaching the gospel but were ultimately freed due to the council's fear of the crowd. Just as Jesus tempered the impulsive Peter without diminishing his courage, Jesus' close relationship with the reflective John encouraged him to develop boldness in preaching the good news of salvation no matter what it cost him. Both knew that, as promised, he would be with them even unto the end of the age (Matt 28:20).

## What can we, as educators, learn from this interaction?

Jesus cultivated a special friendship with the apostle John despite his lack of outspokenness. As teachers, we need to look below the surface of our students' obvious classroom behaviors in order to understand and effectively educate them. Linda Kaplan Thaler and Robin Koval identify several individuals whose unique capabilities were first overlooked.[2] Although initially regarded as quite ordinary in the academic or athletic arena, Steve Jobs, Colin Powell, and Michael Jordan's latent talents were revealed through hard work and determination. Rosa Parks, who identified herself as shy and timid, started the spark of the civil rights movement with her one quiet act of refusing to give up her seat in the white section of a city bus.[3] At first glance, none of these individuals appeared remarkable, but they have all made an impact on the world in their various fields.

In their biographies, intellectual giants Thomas Edison and Albert Einstein were both described as slow in language development and shy in their adult life. Edison, who did not speak until age four, was eventually removed from school and educated by his mother at home.[4] The inventor credited hearing loss as his excuse for not engaging in small talk so as to free himself up to consider ideas instead.[5] Similarly, Einstein said that he thought in ideas and pictures rather than in words.[6] Classroom discussion was certainly not either man's strength, but despite their early schooling experience, these individuals changed history with their extraordinary contributions.

In her book *Quiet: The Power of Introverts in a World That Can't Stop Talking*, Susan Cain researched the profiles of several introverts who have also made outstanding contributions, including Steve Wozniak of Apple, whose creativity was unleashed by working alone over long periods of time.[7] She found that introverts have a harder time than extroverts with change,[8] often requiring gradual transitions over more abrupt ones. But introverts tend to be reflective. They often prefer to make meaning of events rather than participating directly in them. They also prefer to stand out-

2. Kaplan Thaler and Koval, *Grit to Great*, 11–12.
3. Cain, *Quiet*, 2.
4. Stross, *Wizard of Menlo Park*, 4.
5. Ibid., 9.
6. Isaacson, *Einstein*, 8–9.
7. Cain, *Quiet*, 72–73.
8. Ibid., 248.

side of the spotlight but will enter it if they are passionate about the topic being studied.[9]

Cain takes us through home life, schooling, the corporate world, and even evangelical worship services to demonstrate that extroverts are generally preferred in most arenas. Her purpose in doing so is to remind us that introversion is not something to be overcome but is instead at the very core of one-third to one-half of all Americans. As teachers, we need to assure these students that being quiet is a normal and natural quality, not a weakness. Understanding these students may take more effort on our part, but this characteristic is part of who they were created to be.

Knowing our students is not just the task of P-12 teachers. As a professor of education, I have to make predictions about the education students I teach. The ever-present question that permeates my profession is "Does this individual have the knowledge, skills, and dispositions to be an effective teacher?" Because these three categories are enormous in scope, I need to make my decisions based on multiple forms of evidence as demonstrated through my teacher candidates' coursework, clinical experiences, work samples, and informal interactions. I need to know my students well in order to recognize and develop their strengths as well as to remediate their weaknesses.

At times, I've had a wrong first impression of specific teacher candidates who seemed shy in class, but thankfully my colleagues voiced a strength I did not notice. One candidate I thought too timid to be a professional educator ended up teaching in a remote village of Vietnam. Another quiet candidate who seemed too overwhelmed by a suburban class during student teaching ended up thriving in New York City's public schools.

Although all teachers need to be able to communicate and lead well, they do not all need to be strong extroverts. As proven by the students mentioned above, introverted teachers can be effective even in challenging contexts. Ann Myers, a former district superintendent in New York state, recommends that administrators build their faculty and leadership teams with both personality

9. Ibid., 241–63.

types in order to meet the needs of introverted students and to benefit from the different analytical viewpoints that each brings to the profession.[10]

As difficult as it may be for us, particularly at the secondary education level, we need to get to know our quieter, more introverted students in order to understand their personalities and hidden talents. However, we also need to perceive whether their lack of participation in class is due to their basic nature or whether it is emerging as a means of self-protection. I am not inferring that being an introvert is abnormal, since nearly half of our students fall in this category, but I would not want us to attribute a student's withdrawn behavior to being just a personality trait when it could be a possible sign of abuse or a reaction to another form of trauma. C. S. Lewis states, "I have learned now that while those who speak about one's miseries usually hurt, those who keep silence hurt more."[11] This may be the case if we witness a marked behavior change, such as a previously talkative student suddenly becoming reticent in class. Susan Craig has found that students who have experienced trauma may find themselves at a loss for words. Children with such histories may have difficulty using language for solving problems and are sometimes mischaracterized as sullen or defiant, when their lack of speech is merely a response to stress.[12]

With the adoption of Common Core and other state college and career readiness standards that require more collaboration and project-based learning, introverted students may be at a disadvantage in today's classrooms.[13] Although working in small groups and making class presentations have been a part of elementary and secondary education for decades, until recently nearly all assessment of student learning came through individually completed exams or written work. Now a good portion of student evaluation relies upon group participation, a format that makes many intro-

---

10. DeNisco, "Does Common Core Hurt Introverted Students?"

11. Lewis, *Narnia, Cambridge and Joy*, 1102.

12. Craig, *Trauma-Sensitive Schools*, 50.

13. See DeNisco, "Does Common Core Hurt Introverted Students?" and Godsey, "When Schools Overlook Introverts."

verts uncomfortable. This is not surprising, considering that public speaking falls into the top ten of adults' greatest fears on most surveys, usually appearing in the first or second spot on the list.[14]

Cain and Myers hope that educators will not penalize quiet students but will instead balance learning and assessment formats in ways that enable both their extroverted and introverted students to draw upon their strengths. This involves giving students a choice of individual or group assignments and evaluations. It also involves balancing the class period between group and independent work time.

Extroverted traits tend to be more valued in the typical classroom because students with these characteristics are often more responsive to a teacher's instruction. These students are usually the first to answer a question, volunteer for a task, and provide ample feedback on an activity. Teachers know where they stand with these students. Conversely, introverted students are harder to read and therefore require teachers to solicit their participation.

The manner in which teachers engage their shy or quiet students is directly related to their social and academic development. Coplan and Rudasill cite several studies where shy children were more actively engaged in classroom activities with teachers who were sensitive to their needs for a warm and supportive learning climate. Their intentional interaction with this type of student enhanced these students' social interactions with peers as well.[15]

However, a teacher cannot merely cater to the strengths of the introverted student. The reason collaborative learning has been integrated so fully in college and career readiness standards is that most jobs require some form of collaboration. Few occupations allow one to work in solitude throughout the day, so learning to work with and for others is a life skill that all students should develop to some degree.

Teachers can make a significant difference in helping quiet students achieve in their classes. While extroverts seem to be a natural at communication and interpersonal activity, introverts

---

14. Green, "Fear of Public Speaking."
15. Coplan and Rudasill, *Quiet at School*, 66–69.

need structure and scaffolding for collaborative work. Teachers need to put introverts at ease for class presentations by enabling them to rehearse with a peer or small group before standing up in front of the entire class. When holding small-group or whole-class discussions, Myers recommends that teachers have all students write down their thoughts on the topic during the first few minutes of the period.[16] This way, all students are more confident and organized when they present their views orally. Cain also suggests that teachers seat quiet students away from those who are more interactive in order for these quieter students to focus on their work in an environment conducive to their own learning needs.[17] Most importantly, as teachers we need to engage our introverted students not just because they need to develop this aspect of their personality for their future, but also because our learning communities need their insights. Allowing nearly half of our students to opt out of discussions diminishes the quality of the conversation and denies these students an opportunity to be valued for their thinking.

Jonathan Kozol identifies teachers of young children as "specialists in opening small packages." He goes on to say, "They give the string a tug but do it carefully. They don't yet know what's in the box. They don't know if it's breakable."[18] I love this image of teaching that he presents. For our introverted students of any age, their packages are wound with a great deal of string, but inside awaits a wonderful gift.

Jesus recognized John's reflective and expressive abilities and then thoughtfully encouraged him to use these gifts for the kingdom. To teach like a disciple, we must affirm our quiet students for who they are and support their thoughtful contributions.

---

16. DeNisco, "Does Common Core Hurt Introverted Students?"
17. Cain, *Quiet*, 256.
18. Kozol, *Ordinary Resurrections*, 2.

9

# The Provocative Jesus and the Judgmental Student

## Luke 7:36–50

ALTHOUGH THE ACCOUNT OF Jesus and Simon the Pharisee is more commonly known as "A Sinful Woman Anoints Jesus," our focus in this chapter is not on the one who honored Jesus with this act of generosity but rather on the witness to this event, Simon the Pharisee. Jesus was a guest of Simon when a prostitute entered his home in order to express her gratitude to Jesus by lavishing an expensive perfume on his feet. Because of his disdain for the woman, Simon reacted far differently to this act than Jesus did. The contrast between Simon's and Jesus' perception of her has much to teach about how we are to see others whose backgrounds are different from our own and how, as teachers, we can help all our students learn to treat these individuals within and outside our classrooms with respect, particularly those individuals who are a part of vulnerable communities.

### What do we know about Simon?

As a Pharisee, Simon was a leader in the town synagogue, and he had invited Jesus to his home for a meal, most likely after a Sabbath service where Jesus had been teaching.[1] Perhaps Simon's act of hospitality was a custom similar to our present church culture's tradition of pastors inviting guest speakers to their homes for Sunday

---

1. Wenham et al., *New Bible Commentary*, 993.

dinner after the service. In this account, the invitation from Simon may have come out of a sense of obligation, but perhaps he was also engaged by Jesus' teaching or intrigued by Jesus' reputation. Hosting Jesus gave Simon the opportunity to learn more about this prophet from Nazareth.

As a Pharisee, Simon would also have been well educated in the law. He most likely would have also accepted the prevailing cultural view that those who obeyed the law found favor with God and would receive his blessing, while conversely believing that those who did not obey the law or whose parents had not obeyed the law (Num 14:18) failed to gain God's favor and therefore deserved their misfortune in life.[2] This view would certainly assert that a woman with an unfavorable reputation, such as a prostitute, did not deserve God's favor or blessing since she was considered by Old Testament law to be unclean. Because of this distinction, Simon would have needed to avoid touching or interacting with such a woman for fear that he too would become unclean. According to Lev 21:7, prostitution defiled a woman, so you can imagine how upset Simon must have been at having this uninvited guest crash his party and physically touch the guest of honor.

Simon was not only taken aback by the brazenness of this woman, he was equally taken aback by Jesus' response to her. Prior to allowing her to pour perfume on his feet, Jesus had also permitted the woman to wash his feet with her tears, wipe them with her hair, and kiss them, clearly touching him in the process. This response led Simon to discredit Jesus' authority, as evidenced by his thought that "if this man was a prophet, he would know who is touching him and what kind of woman she is—that she is a sinner" (Luke 7:39). Simon thought that since Jesus failed to recognize how inappropriately this woman was behaving toward him, he could not be the knowledgeable and righteous Teacher he claimed to be.

Simon saw the woman as a non-entity through the lens of her profession and her resulting reputation—all the negative labels by which she was known in the community. Instead of a person, he

---

2. Willard, *Divine Conspiracy*, 108.

merely saw moral failure. This perspective dehumanized her. In effect, he was silently asking the teacher, "Jesus, can't you see what kind of person this woman is?"

## What do we know about Jesus from this interaction?

Upon reading this text, I initially wondered why Jesus would have been asked to Simon's home and why Jesus would have accepted Simon's invitation. Didn't Pharisees continually work to discredit Jesus? Didn't Jesus dislike Pharisees? Weren't his harshest words aimed at those teachers of the law who were hypocritical and failed to recognize him as the Messiah? Weren't his most provocative, pointed questions reserved for those whose narrow-mindedness kept them from seeing the truth, as was evident in this Pharisee's reaction to his uninvited guest?

Then I stopped and realized that Jesus avoided prejudicial labels with Simon just as he did with this woman. He did not reject Simon's invitation any more than he did the request for an evening meeting from Nicodemus, another Pharisee. Jesus welcomed the opportunity to engage with Simon. He saw potential in Simon. I was the one guilty of narrow-mindedness by assuming the worst in Simon and failing to see him as someone who could learn from Jesus. Jesus was far more open-minded than I was regarding this student.

In the field of education, we use Jacob Kounin's term "withitness" to describe a teacher's ability to monitor and interpret student behavior throughout the entire classroom.[3] Withitness requires frequently observing all students in order to determine if they are on- or off-task and to assess how their actions reveal their attitudes toward learning. This is particularly challenging when a teacher is working with an individual student while the rest of the class is expected to work independently, because this requires balancing the needs of the group against attending to the demands of instructing the individual. The purpose of withitness is to detect or

---

3. Kounin, *Discipline and Group Management*, 74–91.

foresee any off-task behavior in order to redirect it. A teacher with a strong sense of withitness will eventually prevent most off-task behavior from occurring, since students expect that they will be called out for failing to do what they need to be doing. As a result, they get to work right away. Because of this effect, withitness is a valuable skill for teachers. It requires the perception and anticipation of students' behaviors and attitudes.

Jesus had a remarkable sense of withitness not only in perceiving the motivation behind both Simon's and the woman's actions, but also in sensing Simon's unvoiced criticism. It is the same ability we see in Mark 2:1–12 when Jesus addressed the Pharisees' unvoiced accusations at his healing of the paralyzed man. In this case, however, Jesus chose to help Simon realize his own error rather than confront him directly about his prejudicial perspective. Jesus recognized a teachable moment for a teacher of the law. He gently informed Simon that he had something to tell him. As a result, Simon was receptive and asked Jesus to continue.

Jesus was not influenced by cultural assumptions or social conventions, which in this case would have required him to rebuke or at least ignore the woman. To help Simon understand his unexpected response to her kindness, Jesus created a personal parable for Simon. He described a situation in which one person owed ten times as much to a money lender as another borrower. Neither of the borrowers was able to repay his debt, but the lender amazingly pardoned both of them. Jesus then asked Simon which of the two debtors would love the lender more for forgiving the burden of the debt. Simon hesitatingly replied, "I suppose the one who had the bigger debt" (Luke 7:43).

Perhaps this revelation helped Simon recognize his own misperception. Jesus reinforced this lesson by stating, "You have *judged* correctly." I think he chose this verb specifically because Simon's animosity toward the woman was based on his prior judgment of her.

One might think that Jesus' question "Now which of them will love him more?" was the more provocative question Jesus posed, but he asked this question in order to prepare Simon for the key question that followed. In truth, Jesus asked aloud the very same question that Simon's thinking had implied: "Simon, do you see this woman? Do you *really* see this woman—not her labels or her past sins—but do you see this woman as *I* see her?"

Jesus connected the principle from his parable to his interaction with the woman by asking Simon to compare the reception he had given Jesus to the one the woman had just given him. Simon had welcomed Jesus into his home and hosted him for a meal but did not offer to have Jesus' feet washed. In contrast, the woman had washed Jesus' dusty feet with her tears, wiped them dry with her hair, anointed them with perfume, and kissed them. Although Simon did nothing wrong in his actions as host, Jesus pointed out to Simon what he did *not* do in order to help him see that the woman's extraordinary outpouring of gratitude was based on what Jesus' redemption had accomplished in her life. His prior forgiveness had absolved her of her debt of sin and made possible the transformation of her life from one of sin to one of obedience. Her expression of devotion toward her pardoner revealed her essence far more accurately than her labels or reputation. Jesus' learning goal for Simon was to have him see the woman for who she truly was. This was how Jesus saw her.

But Jesus didn't end his lesson there. He had a second objective for Simon to learn, as he revealed by saying, "But whoever has been forgiven little loves little" (Luke 7:47). This implied that Simon's pride affected his relationship with God. The very position Simon took to assure himself that he was in good standing with Jehovah prevented him from having any positive standing whatsoever. He too needed to seek forgiveness from the Messiah, God's only Son.

## What can we learn from Simon?

If we are not careful, we could end up seeing Simon as inaccurately as he saw the woman. We could let our own prejudices lead us to regard him as little more than a self-righteous, arrogant leader without any redeeming potential. But Jesus didn't dismiss Simon this way any more than he dismissed the sinful woman. He didn't treat him as a lost cause. Instead, he accepted Simon's invitation to dinner. He took the time to reach out to Simon and helped him understand the concept of grace, perhaps for the first time in his life.

Simon initially saw humankind in two camps, those who had earned God's favor and those who had not. This favor was largely determined by a level of observed obedience. Like the Pharisee in Jesus' parable (Luke 18:9–14) who saw himself as superior to the remorse-filled publican (i.e., tax collector), Simon saw himself as more valuable to God than the uninvited woman. To Simon, she belonged in the publican's camp, undeserving of his and Jesus' regard. Simon viewed his own sins as small in comparison to hers. As a result, he needed very little forgiveness from God. He lived a life of privilege, and up until he met Jesus, he believed he had come to deserve the privileges he experienced through his own merit.

Unfortunately for Simon, Scripture tells us that God does not operate in a comparative economy. He does not rescue those who barely need his mercy and then abandon those who require too much from him. God does not see us this way. As we read in Rom 3:23, "For *all* have sinned and fall short of the glory of God." This group ranges from the most meticulous Pharisee to the woman whose life is entrenched in sin. It is not how much we have sinned that determines if we need a Savior but rather the fact that we have sinned at all. We find this sad truth confirmed in Rom 3:10: "There is none that is righteous, no not one." We are all in need of God's grace and forgiveness.

However, by this statement I do not wish to infer that obedience is unimportant to God; all of Scripture contradicts this implication. But it is not our obedience that saves us. We cannot earn God's favor. We must realize that we are helpless to save ourselves and rely solely on Jesus' atonement for our salvation. Our obedience is expected after forgiveness, but like the woman's gift of perfume, it comes out of gratitude for the grace he has extended toward us.

## The Provocative Jesus and the Judgmental Student

It would be easy to condemn Simon for his mistaken sense of superiority, but then we must ask ourselves if we have ever been guilty of this same perspective. Do we see ourselves as better than Simon and therefore needing only a little forgiveness? Perhaps we slip into this perspective in ways we don't even realize.

I remember being on our church music committee when a woman who sang more from her heart than from talent asked to perform a solo in a Sunday morning service. Knowing the limitations of the singer's voice, the committee invited her to sing instead during an evening service when fewer would be in attendance. I know this is not the place to debate the wisdom of this decision, but I couldn't help wondering as I left the meeting, "To God's ear, don't we all sound like her? Don't we all fall short of the angelic choirs?"

I am reminded of this event every time I read Ps 19:14, "May these words of my mouth and this meditation of my heart be pleasing in your sight, LORD, my Rock and my Redeemer." This verse reminds me that we need to ask God to accept our humble voices because without this request, their sound would not be worthy of his audience. Although there are certainly times when we need to hold to clearly established standards, too often we draw arbitrary lines to identify who is acceptable and who is not. And most often that line divides people into camps of those who are just like us and those who are not.

Although we don't know for certain whether Simon became a follower of Christ, we can see Simon's journey toward truth in this account as he comprehended Jesus' parable and its application. Perhaps he did come to follow Christ and later relayed this account to Luke for inclusion in his gospel. Jesus' provocative question of "Do you see this woman?" and his provocative comment, "But whoever has been forgiven little, loves little," gave Simon much to think about long after Jesus had left his house. It gives us much to think about as well.

## What can we learn from Jesus in this interaction?

Jesus' classroom that day included two students from opposite ends of the learning spectrum. He had a student who thought he knew it all and had already aced the final exam. But this was a very inaccurate self-assessment. Not only was Simon's view of himself incorrect, he used himself as the moral measuring stick for all other individuals. He regarded the woman who had entered his home as unworthy of his time or regard. His contempt for this woman was easily read by the Master Teacher, who saw her in a very different light. Jesus responded rather provocatively to Simon's expectations. He not only engaged the woman in conversation, he also allowed her to touch him. Simon was shocked that Jesus viewed this sinful woman differently than he himself had viewed her.

Jesus next provoked Simon's thinking by asking him to judge which of the two forgiven debtors would be most grateful and then provoked the Pharisee to reexamine his behavior by challenging him to see this woman differently than he had before this transformative moment. Finally, Jesus challenged Simon's assessment of his own commitment to God by equating one's desire for mercy with one's depth of devotion. Only those who saw their great need for God's forgiveness could fully appreciate his love for them. Out of this knowledge came an intense desire to repent, to worship, and to serve him.

On the other end of the learning spectrum is the woman. Her initial response to Jesus was a flood of tears. Coming from a profession that required her to pretend an artificial affection for men who objectified her, she met Jesus, who may have been the first man to show her genuine love. Out of her enslavement, he offered her freedom. Out of her self-contempt, he offered her respect. Out of her degradation, he offered her dignity.

Her tears could have come from remorse over this past or they could have come from her memory of the present. Just a few days or hours prior to this encounter she had heard Jesus' message of hope and forgiveness. Through faith, she believed in who he was and recognized her need for repentance.

Her tears may have also been, in part, a result of Simon's reaction to her. Unlike the woman who touched Jesus' garment, this woman's restoration was private. No one else may have known of her repentance except Jesus. As a result, she would likely still experience the loathsome stares of the righteous and the jeers of her former clients. Her future was uncertain in the community; she was still economically, socially, and spiritually vulnerable.

Why, then, would she risk entering Simon's home to thank Jesus? I think her bravery came from the same place as Mary Magdalene's courage when she stood by Jesus at the cross, prepared his body for burial, and sought to claim his body at the empty tomb. Both women had known how desolate their lives were before they met Jesus and had experienced an immediate transformation because of his healing and forgiveness. They were totally committed to him despite the price they might be required to pay for their devotion. Given their backgrounds, I can understand and admire their amazing level of courage.

I love the instructive conclusion of this story. Jesus assured the woman that her sins were forgiven and then reminded her that it was her faith in him that had saved her. Her forgiveness was certainly not due to her obedience or any other human action that Simon would have believed necessary to receive it. This brief confirmation that Jesus offered the woman was just as much for Simon's benefit as her own. For her, redemption through faith offered hope; for Simon, it offered a radically different theology.

Jesus concluded his remarks to the woman by telling her to go in peace. When you and I hear the benediction "Go in peace" at the end of a service, we probably cannot understand this blessing's impact in the same degree this woman did. Her life had been anything but peaceful. Up until that point, she had been demoralized and dehumanized on a daily basis, but now her Savior had told her to go in peace. Now that her community had learned of her repentance, peace was possible.

Most of us take peace for granted, but this is not every believer's experience. A believer living in a country hostile to Christianity does not take peace for granted. Neither does a young child walking to school in Chicago's Englewood neighborhood as she wonders whether she will return home or be killed by a stray bullet. A middle school student with a physical disability may not take peace for granted as he navigates the hallways between classes and hears cruel comments from his peers. There are many places where peace is only an aspiration and not a reality. And there are many places that need us to advocate for peace on behalf of others.

Simon had one more objective to learn from Jesus. He needed to understand that Jesus was whom he claimed to be, the promised Messiah and Redeemer of the world. Only then could Simon recognize that Jesus had the power to forgive sins. The woman had understood and accepted this truth, but Simon had not. This lesson had to be far more difficult for him than for her because it required him to reject his prior worldview, which had been built on self-righteousness, and replace it with total dependence on God's mercy. All his previous effort would not count for anything. In a realm whose leader preached "Those who are last now will be first then, and those who are first will be last" (Matt 20:16), Simon had much to lose. The necessary shift in his thinking was monumental, but ultimately he had everything to gain.

## What can we, as educators, learn from this interaction?

In this account, we see Jesus stepping into a role that all teachers must inhabit from time to time, the role of advocate. We first see Jesus advocating for the woman's protection. By allowing the woman to touch him, Jesus signaled to Simon that he would defend her. Jesus showed the woman that she was physically and emotionally safe with him. But Jesus also saw his responsibility to help Simon accept her. Good teachers not only model acceptance of unpopular students, they also establish clear guidelines that others must do the same. Jesus did this not by confronting Simon but by gently teaching him.

One of the most effective models of advocating for vulnerable students I've experienced was an urban middle school language arts teacher who began the year by taking down the lengthy poster of official school rules from her classroom wall and replacing it with one that contained only one sentence: "You will be safe here."[4] She and her sixth-grade students formed a caring learning community through reading novels that focused on children during World War II whose safety was similarly threatened. In discussing the main characters of Lois Lowry's *Number the Stars*, Uri Orlev's *The Island on Bird Street*, and Eleanor Coerr's *Sadako and the Thousand Paper Cranes*, her students found solace from the unsafe streets of their Chicago neighborhood. Her one-sentence expectation for every student ensured that they would not only refrain from mistreating each other but would support one another as well. In establishing this kind of classroom atmosphere, she served as a peacemaker to her students living in difficult times.

Diverse student populations enrich the learning experience for everyone, but not all students enter a classroom seeing it this way. Many students are prejudiced against classmates with different racial, political, religious, linguistic or family backgrounds as well as those with different physical and emotional disabilities, sexual orientation, or economic resources. This dislike surfaces in classroom discussions in forms ranging from subtle remarks to open hostility. Behaviors can range from micro-aggressions to outright bullying. This is not behavior we, as Christian educators, can ignore.

When faced with a student who is disrespectful of a classmate or a group of individuals within or outside of class, it can be tempting to offer a searing comment that would humble the student or confront the antagonist in a way that belittles him or her. But by doing so, we become a bully ourselves. Jesus gently informed Simon that he had something to tell him. Because of Jesus' wise approach, Simon was receptive and asked the Master Teacher to continue. However, advocating in a calm and quiet way still requires authority. We cannot merely request that our students treat each other fairly; we must demand it by communicating clear expectations and consequences for those who fail to meet them.

4. Lederhouse, "You Will Be Safe Here," 51–54.

Sometimes the students who most need to see the harmful effect of their preconceptions are not those sitting in our classrooms but are actually our fellow faculty members. Their dislike for a student, subtle or otherwise, may not be due to demographic prejudices. It may be directed against a student whose siblings or parents have a reputation for being difficult.

At other times, we ourselves may be the ones who inhabit the role of Simon. As a Christian teacher in a public or even a private school, we will undoubtedly work with some students and families whose values and life choices are quite different from our own. We must intentionally and repeatedly examine our own hearts to ensure that we respect students who do not share our core beliefs and enable them to feel a sense of welcome in our classes. We must daily ask the Lord to help us see each student as he sees them.

Like some of our colleagues, we can similarly fall into the trap of dreading having to work with specific students, particularly if we lack appropriate resources for helping them. We may also be anxious about interacting with parents and guardians who have a history of being overly involved or uninvolved with their child's learning. One of the Christian teachers I had the pleasure of working with shared a wonderful way to transform this fear of working with these children, parents, or guardians into a sense of calling. Instead of worrying about potentially demanding students or parents in next year's class, she started the practice of praying for them even before she said goodbye to her current class in June. Throughout the summer, she continued to pray for the students and families the Lord chose for her to help in the coming school year. It didn't change them; it changed her attitude about working with them. From that point on, she said she never saw a student or family as one to be tolerated until year's end; she didn't dread parent conferences with them. Instead, she saw each family as directed to her by God. She felt responsible for giving each of them the best year of their academic life.

Soon this transformation of attitude became apparent to her coworkers. Her principal commented to me that no one else in his school worked more effectively with "challenging" children or parents. He said that every parent he knew was delighted to get this teacher because they knew their children would be treated fairly and that they were always welcome in her classroom. This teacher's prayers turned her anxiety into her mission and passion.

Early in my career as a primary specialist who worked with struggling young learners, I would participate in meetings to determine whether individual students were eligible for special education services. These meetings, of course, included parents who frequently showed subtle signs of emotional distress upon hearing the results of their child's evaluation. They would often tear up and disengage from the conversation as they tried to process what these recommendations would mean for their child's future.

Occasionally, a colleague would miss these signals and just continue to highlight the academic skills that were expected by this time but that the child was unable to perform. Thankfully, I had a perceptive administrator who would interrupt the evaluator to ask parents if they could use another cup of coffee. This imposed break showed my colleague that she had overstated her case. It also helped me learn my role. My purpose became to highlight all that the child *could* do and state why I enjoyed working with him or her. These parents needed some hope and some sign that they had a wonderful child despite these academic or social weaknesses.

This experience taught me that there is truly something winsome about every child. It may not be an academic strength, but there is always some quality—a quirky sense of humor, a display of enthusiasm, or a consistent politeness—that makes us grateful to be with them. On some days, we may need to remind our other students, our colleagues, or even ourselves of these gifts, but they are present in these children all the same. We must remember that the student who faces unjust treatment, no matter the source of that antagonism, is the one who most needs our protection and advocacy.

I think of Ps 3:1–3 as the psalm for students with special needs:

> O Lord, how many are my foes! How many rise up against me. Many are saying of me, "God will not deliver

him." But you are a shield around me, O Lord; you bestow glory on me and lift up my head.

I have always read this psalm at the start of my special education course and ask my pre-service teachers if they will be among those who rise up against these students or if they will stand as their shield. Will they join the chorus that expects these children to fail or will they lift up their head? I ask if they will act as a protector and advocate against those who see their students as less deserving. To teach like a disciple, we must help the Simons of this world see others as Jesus sees them.

# 10

# The Purposeful Jesus and the Students Who Wanted Him to Please Them

## *John 11:1–57*

JOHN'S ACCOUNT OF THE raising of Lazarus chronicles the greatest miracle Jesus performed up until his own death and resurrection: bringing a man who had been dead for four days back to life again. Although Jesus learned of Lazarus' illness early enough to have reached the sick man before he succumbed to death, Jesus chose instead to wait until after Lazarus had died before traveling to his home. When Jesus finally arrived there, he spoke with both grieving sisters, Mary and Martha, and then asked to visit the burial site of his friend. Upon reaching the tomb, Jesus called to Lazarus, miraculously raising him from the dead to the amazement of all who witnessed the event.

Although most of us read the familiar story already knowing the glorious outcome for Lazarus and his family, we can fail to realize that Jesus' delay came with a cost. He had to know beforehand the physical and emotional consequences of deferring his visit. We know from studying his other encounters that Jesus cared deeply for people, so it seems out of character for him to be so unresponsive to his close friends Lazarus, Mary, and Martha. The women had sent word that their brother was seriously ill in the expectation that Jesus would come right away in order to heal him. He had done this for strangers, so why shouldn't they expect that he would immediately set out for Bethany?

Jesus, however, purposefully waited two more days before making the journey to the home of Lazarus and his sisters. If he could feed 5,000 strangers, why would he seemingly deny his miraculous power to those he knew well and loved? Even the distance between geographic areas should not have been an obstacle to helping his dear friends. Just as he assured the Capernaum official in Cana that his son back home was healed, surely he could have similarly restored Lazarus back to health from his remote location, but he did not. What does this intentional postponement have to teach us as believers, and what insights does it hold for us about our own role as educators?

## What do we know about Martha and Mary?

We know from another gospel writer that these two sisters had previously shown hospitality to Jesus. Luke records the conversation Martha had with Jesus when she and her sister had entertained him earlier in their home (Luke 10:38–42). At that time, she complained to the Lord that Mary was not helping her serve their guests but instead was just sitting and listening to him. Rather than agreeing with Martha, Jesus defended Mary's action, telling Martha that her sister had made a better choice.

What is significant about his response is that it gives validity to women being disciples of Jesus. They had an equal right to be his students along with men. Jesus did not relegate women to the kitchen but instead welcomed them to hear his teaching in the same way he invited men. I am sure that Martha was surprised by his response to her complaint.

John refers to Mary in the second verse of chapter 11 as the one who poured expensive perfume on Jesus' feet and wiped them with her hair. Although this event did not occur until after Lazarus was raised (John 12:3), the gospel writer identifies her in this way, according to Gundry,[1] to distinguish her from other women named Mary who were also followers of Jesus. Mary's subsequent action was performed out of gratitude for what Jesus had done for her family—giving them back her brother. Although this reference

---

1. Gundry, *Commentary on the New Testament*, 410.

## Jesus and the Students Who Wanted Him to Please Them

is out of sequence, John makes this point of clarification for the benefit of the reader. Mary's sacrificial act of gratitude reflected how deeply she cared for Jesus. This family loved him.

These siblings from Bethany were probably well known in the area because many Jews—some of whom undoubtedly hailed from nearby Jerusalem—came to mourn Lazarus after his death and console the two women. The house was crowded with visitors. As a result, Martha was probably busy feeding them while Mary was too distraught to react to the news that Jesus was arriving outside the village gate.

Martha got word of Jesus' approach and left her house to meet him, greeting him with the heartfelt but confident statement, "Lord, if you had been here, my brother wouldn't have died. Nevertheless, I know that even now God will give you anything you ask." Despite her sorrow, she recognized that Jesus was no ordinary teacher or human being. He was equipped with divine power, including power over death. Even in her suffering, she believed him to be who he said he was and clung to the hope he had given her.

When Jesus assured her by saying, "Your brother will rise again," she responded, "I know he will rise again in the resurrection at the last day." Despite failing to win Jesus' support for getting Mary to help her in the kitchen, Martha had obviously listened to Jesus, either at his feet with her sister or while preparing his meal, because she had learned her theology well. Although grief-stricken and heartbroken over his timing, Martha affirmed Jesus' teaching and trusted him. Her faith in him was stronger than her disappointment.

In verse twenty-five of the passage, Jesus claimed that he is the Resurrection and the Life and that no one who believes in him will ever die an eternal death. When he asked her by name if she believed this, Martha replied, "Yes, Lord, I have come to believe that you are the Messiah, the Son of God, the one who is coming into the world." Even great personal tragedy—tragedy that she believed he could have prevented—did not dissuade her from this truth.

Jesus and Martha were not referring to an afterlife of "resting in Jesus." Gundry reminds us that the word "resurrection" means "the standing up."[2] It is a bodily resurrection, not just the awakening of the soul. Martha and Jesus were discussing the actual reanimation of the physical person. Even though her brother appeared lost to her, Martha's conversation showed that she still believed Jesus had the power to rescue him.

While Martha was a woman of action and went immediately to greet Jesus, Mary needed some prompting from her sister before she left home to go out to see him. She was hurt by his apparent disregard of their call for help and only went when Jesus personally asked her to come. She may have waited to face him, but when Martha summoned her, Mary went quickly. Assuming she was headed to the tomb, the mourners followed her.

When Mary saw Jesus outside the village, she fell at his feet and poured out her hurt and anger by saying, "Lord, if you had been here, my brother would not have died." Jesus saw and heard all her pain in that accusation, for it implied, "Why, why, *why* didn't you get here on time?" John writes that several of the mourners asked why Jesus, who had healed a blind man, could not have prevented Lazarus' death. I am sure they only voiced what Mary must have been thinking. She wept brokenly, and this resulted in Jesus himself weeping. Jesus felt these sisters' heartache and loss.

## What do we know about Jesus from this interaction?

I believe the most significant descriptor of Jesus in this passage is found in verse five: "Jesus loved Martha and her sister and Lazarus." He cared deeply about this family. He knew them well and understood the depth of their faith in him—a faith that would be severely tested during this encounter. He had been to their home and had formed a strong bond with them. He had confronted Martha yet still had her loyalty, which would only be possible if they

---

2. Ibid., 412.

had established a strong relationship. While others had deserted him, these three still believed in him. They were like family to him.

We also know from the beginning of the story that Jesus knew Lazarus' outcome before Jesus left for Bethany. He knew that Lazarus would live again and that many would believe Jesus was the Son of God as a result of miraculously raising his friend from the dead. He knew that ultimately God would be glorified in Lazarus' bodily resurrection through the salvation of the eyewitnesses and in the ultimate salvation of the cross. Christ had this long-term goal in sight when he delayed his trip to help his friends.

However, he also understood the toll this delay would exact from these friends. They, of course, would only view the event in the short term. They would be utterly disappointed in him. Lazarus would suffer physically, and his sisters would suffer emotionally. Jesus knew ahead of time what it would cost them.

Jesus also knew another significant result of this miracle. As we read at the chapter's conclusion, this event triggered the call for his own arrest, trial, and death (John 11:45–57). Reports of this miracle filtered back to the Pharisees and resulted in a meeting of the Sanhedrin. At that event, Caiaphas, the high priest, called for Jesus' execution, and the Jewish leaders developed a plan to end Jesus' life.

We have evidence in this chapter that Jesus and his disciples were aware of the hostility from Jewish leaders against him. John 11:8 records his disciples' objections to heading back to Judea because of a prior attempt on his life by stoning. But verse sixteen also reflects Thomas' commitment to Jesus despite this hostility. He stated, "Let us also go, that we may die with him." Jesus knowingly went to Lazarus and brought him back to life even though this decision would soon result in his own death by crucifixion.

Finally, Jesus understood one more important aspect of this event. He understood his mission. He was not sent from the Father merely to teach, heal, and perform other miracles. He was sent to do more than supernaturally help others with physical trials. His mission was to win a history-altering, spiritual battle against the powers of sin and darkness. He was to do the work of his Father, no matter what the cost. Nothing was more important than accomplishing his assignment. When he uttered the words "It is finished" on the cross, he was not referring to his life but his work. He had obeyed the Father and surrendered his own life for our redemption. Nothing could dissuade him from this mission, not even doing what his dearest friends had asked him to do.

## What can we learn from Martha and Mary?

The gospels give us stark contrasts between these two sisters. I am quite confident that Martha was the older of the two women by virtue of her personality and sense of responsibility. She was the one in charge of their home, while Mary was her reluctant assistant. Martha was a person accustomed to action. She seemed to be the kind of person described in the familiar statement "If you want something done, give it to a busy person." She likely checked off a pretty impressive to-do list each day. I would imagine she was the chair of the fellowship committee at her synagogue and probably the head of every volunteer organization in Bethany with her type-A, task-oriented personality. She likely did everything and did it well. She is characterized by Bruner as the practical and resilient sister.[3]

On the other hand, Mary appears to be the contemplative sister, with her type-B, people-oriented personality. I think it would have been hard to be Mary, competing as she must have had to with such an accomplished older sister in Martha. Although she may have been quieter, Mary was not necessarily submissive. My guess is that her refusal to help Martha when Jesus and the disciples visited was not the first conflict between the two sisters. I doubt Martha would have called on Jesus to advocate for her plan if this issue was not a long-standing problem between the two women. Mary was a risk-taker in challenging Martha's more traditional role for women by leaving the kitchen to enter Jesus' "classroom." Unlike her exasperated sister, who put on the coffee

---

3. Bruner, *Gospel of John*, 666.

and set the table when guests arrived, Mary showed hospitality by listening to them.

Because Mary valued spending time with others over catering to their physical needs, the loss of her brother and her disappointment in Jesus were especially difficult for her. She was heartbroken. It is interesting to note that the two sisters confronted Jesus with the identical statement, "Lord, if you'd been here, my brother would not have died." But Martha followed her greeting with a message of confidence and hope, "But I know that even now God will give you whatever you ask." Her response prompted Jesus to assure her that he was the source of life; he held the power of resurrection within him. However, after Mary gave the same opening statement, she broke down weeping—she was inconsolable. Her raw and honest response moved Jesus to tears.

From Martha, we learn that our faith can support us in times of sorrow. Her confidence in the person of Jesus focused her on the future—a future of hope. Her faith in Christ was stronger than her disappointment in her friend's failure to heal her brother. Bruner writes that Martha's answer to Jesus' question was based on her relationship with him.[4] She did not separate the claims of Christ from the person of Christ. She trusted him, so she believed what he was saying.

From Mary, we learn that we can be honest with God. There was no judgment in Christ's response to her, only empathy. She poured out her heart to him, and he accepted her. Like David in the psalms, she communicated her hurt and frustration with God's lack of response. David wrote in Ps 10:1, "Why, Lord, do you stand off? Why do you hide yourself in times of trouble?" In Ps 6, David's lament tells of his tears flooding his bed all night long, and in Ps 42:3, he writes of being a downcast soul whose tears "have been my food day and night." He used prayer to communicate honestly with his Creator.

From Mary, we also learn that we don't have to pretend to be perfect before God. Jesus himself said, "Come to me, all you who are weary and burdened, and I will give you rest" (Matt 11:28).

4. Ibid., 667.

Prayer is an opportunity for us to release our burdens and give them over to the Lord, who will comfort us. In his first letter, the Apostle Peter encouraged fellow believers to "Cast all your anxiety on him because he cares for you" (1 Pet 5:7). However, we can't turn over our worries to Jesus without first identifying them. Because of what he has done for us and because of the concern he showed Mary, we can come to him with our deepest heartaches, greatest disappointments, and our gravest worries with the confidence that he will hear us.

Mary also teaches us that when Christ calls, we need to respond to him. Although she was grieving the loss of her brother and was utterly disappointed in Jesus' failure to prevent his death, she still went to him when he asked for her. I imagine it was emotionally difficult for her to leave her home, but her relationship with the Teacher was solid enough to overcome these hard circumstances. She may have been tempted to refuse Jesus' request, but we don't find her bitter or despondent. John writes that she went to him quickly.

## What can we learn from Jesus in this interaction?

Although I do not want to diminish the wonder of Christ's power to bring someone back from the dead, this is not a spiritual insight that has much practical value for us as educators. (The challenge of raising the dead does not fall under normal teaching responsibilities unless, of course, you have had to teach a 7:30 a.m. class.) Yes, we have a relationship with the Savior of the world, who is the Resurrection and the Life. Yes, we have access to someone who always knows our circumstances and provides us with the Holy Spirit, who enables us to remain faithful because of or in spite of them. These are essential truths that are embedded in this passage. Yet another major lesson we can learn from Jesus in this interaction is that he often has a different timetable than we have for our requests.

I remember praying for wisdom in my first semester of teaching. My urban classroom had thirty-seven first graders, only one of whom was reading when I entered their classroom in February. Despite my hard work, I was often overwhelmed by their needs and my inability to meet them effectively. Each day, I would ask God for many improvements in my teaching and my children's learning; in essence, I wanted the ability to teach as an experienced educator. This was a prayer he could not answer. I needed time to understand my students and their parents in order to develop strong relationships with them. I needed time to understand my curriculum in order to differentiate it effectively. I needed time to transform my romantic notion of teaching into one based on reality. This expertise did not come in a day or even weeks but grew over many months and years.

God's timetable was quite different than mine. My prayer to become an instant super-teacher was gradually replaced by a prayer to see my students as he would see them. He saw the long-term goal when I only saw my short-term needs. My prayer was answered, though not as immediately as I desired. I wanted to avoid the countless mistakes I ended up making that first semester, but I had to experience them. On a daily basis, I found that developing expertise in one's profession can be a slow and painful process.

Although this biblical narrative includes many significant benefits from Jesus' timing, I don't know if, in retrospect, Mary, Martha, and especially Lazarus would have chosen to be part of this spectacular miracle if they had been given the option. In a small way, I can relate to this family whose members paid a high price for each of their roles in the event. After my high school-aged daughter was diagnosed with cancer, I was told by a well-meaning individual that someday she would have a powerful testimony as a result of her experience. At the time, the remark only angered me. In my perspective, the cost of going through the emotional strain and physical ordeal of several surgeries, multiple treatments, and countless scans was far too high for this spiritual outcome. Despite receiving God's abundant grace through those years and having a healthy daughter today, I can honestly say that I still would never have chosen that journey for my family. Even knowing today that this trial turned out well for us, it came with a significant price. Recognizing that illness is a part of living in a fallen world, I never blamed God for our circumstances or even questioned him about it, but I would never have volunteered our family for such an ordeal. Therefore, I can empathize with the Bethany sisters. As a result of my own family's experience, I am grateful to John for including in his subsequent chapter Martha and Mary's acts of gratitude to Jesus for restoring their brother (John 12:2–3). I need this conclusion to learn from their examples of how to respond to the hard aspects of life.

The second lesson we learn from Jesus is related to the first. Jesus knew how difficult his delay would be for the Bethany family, but it did not change his plan. He was fully aware of what the two sisters wanted him to do, yet he deliberately chose not to come when they called him. Unlike many leaders of his and our day, Jesus could not be characterized as a people-pleaser. He had more important work to do. He loved this family, but he was mission-focused over everything else. He formed his timetable to align with his Father's purpose, not his friends'.

This is not a comforting statement, because it not only means we may not get what we want from Jesus at the time we want it, we may not ever get what we want. Jesus is not our personal shopper or problem-solver. He is not in the same business as Amazon; we cannot just order what we want and expect it delivered to our doorsteps within three to five business days. His assurances in Scripture about granting whatever we ask are all contingent upon his purposes. Psalm 37:4 states, "Take delight in the LORD, and he will give you the desires of your heart." Jesus' promise in Matt 7:7, "Ask and it will be given to you," follows his teachings on being obedient and committed followers. Jesus promised the disciples that they would receive what they asked for only if they remained in him (John 15:7). In his first letter, John states that whatever we ask for must be according to his will (1 John 5:14). God's primary purpose is not to give us an easy life. His promises are written as an assurance that he will equip us for his work.

JESUS AND THE STUDENTS WHO WANTED HIM TO PLEASE THEM

## What can we, as educators, learn from this interaction?

All teachers, but especially novices, want their students to like them. This desire is healthy and even necessary to the profession. Educators cannot understand their students' academic needs and interests without establishing and maintaining positive interactions with them. These constructive relationships are essential to creating an inviting learning environment.[5]

The opportunity to develop meaningful relationships with students is often what draws us to the profession. If you have ever encountered an educator who didn't appear to like people, you probably wondered why he or she even entered teaching. And if you had to learn from one of these teachers, your experience may have even negatively affected your regard for the content he or she taught. The type of rapport teachers establish has serious consequences for learning.

While I want to validate the desire to be liked as a normal and positive disposition for teaching, this desire can create challenges, especially for inexperienced teachers. We cannot seek to be liked at the expense of student learning. Few novice teachers arrive in the classroom with the same perspective as Esmé Codell, who chronicled her first year of teaching in the book *Educating Esmé*. Her January 11 entry describes her experience observing a disastrous lesson taught by the school's special education teacher.[6] This teacher, who was well known among all the students for managing her individual students' behavior through tangible rewards, entered Esmé's classroom to teach the whole class a math lesson while Esmé worked in the back of the room. Yet the students quickly became disruptive when one student rudely asked what reward they would get for doing as she instructed. When the young special education teacher surprisingly offered stickers, Esmé could not hold her tongue. "What'll you get? What'll you *get*? You'll get

5. Marzano, Marzano, and Pickering, *Classroom Management*, 41.
6. Codell, *Educating Esmé*, 86–87.

an education! That's what you'll get!" she interrupted.[7] In tears after class, the young special education teacher admitted that she just wanted the students to like her. "It's not our job to be liked," Esmé wisely reminded her. "It's our job to help them be smart."[8]

Similarly, it is our job to be firm—not mean, but firm. These are not synonymous terms. Our academic and behavioral expectations must be clear, firmly established, and consistently applied.

Although most beginning teachers are sure that their desire to have students like them will never interfere with their students' learning, novices are often unaware of how their interaction can lead to scenarios similar to that experienced by this special education teacher, whom Esmé describes by saying, "The kids eat her alive."[9] Young teachers often fail to realize that students need boundaries and structure in order to feel secure. The absence of clearly established rules and procedures leaves students confused and ill at ease. Even with established rules, a teacher's failure to follow through with consequences or interventions for disregarding those rules frequently leads to inappropriate learning behaviors.

Working primarily to please our students is a fruitless and detrimental goal. Teachers who consciously or subconsciously make this their priority only end up disappointing their students and themselves. Although this insight may be somewhat intuitive, research has indicated that leniency on homework, course requirements, or deadlines has a negative impact on learning.[10] Other studies on teacher effectiveness have clearly demonstrated the relationship between setting high standards and student achievement at all levels of schooling.[11] What may earn short-term relational points in the present only results in academic and relational shortcomings in the future.

7. Ibid., 87.
8. Ibid.
9. Ibid., 86.
10. Brooks, "Teacher Leniency/Strictness."
11. See Haycock, "Good Teaching Matters"; Marzano, Marzano, and Pickering, *Classroom Management*; Wright, Horn, and Sanders, "Teacher and Classroom Context."

Trying to be the cool teacher does not serve students well. Because we are professionals, we need a bigger goal. As with any relationship, we cannot build rapport with students based on a pattern of making concessions to our students. Jesus' relationship with Mary, Martha, and Lazarus has much to offer us in terms of balancing our personal need for affirmation against our professional focus. To teach like a disciple, we need to choose our mission over pleasing our students.

11

# The Transforming Jesus and the Student No One Believed in

## Acts 9:1–31, Phil 3:4–6

NO FOLLOWER OF CHRIST had a greater transformation than the Apostle Paul. Not only did he initially reject Jesus as the Messiah, he also persecuted and killed those who followed him. But Jesus saw great potential in Paul and began his education by confronting him with the truth of his divine nature on a Damascus road.

Because of Paul's prior campaign against Christ's followers, it was logical that even after his conversion, the apostles were afraid of him. However, two believers, Ananias and Barnabas, though skeptical at first, soon came to believe in Paul's genuine transformation. They stood by Paul, trusting him, educating him, and advocating for him to the others. Their investment in Paul had an incredible return for the kingdom.

### What do we know about Paul?

During my time as a department chair at a Christian liberal arts college, I oversaw faculty searches for eight full-time positions. As part of this process, I spent many hours matching numerous applicants' credentials against our selection criteria. Unlike heading a teacher preparation program at a large university where a faculty member might teach several sections of only one education course, I needed to find candidates to join our relatively small department who could teach and oversee programs in more than one major area, such as historical and philosophical foundations as well as secondary education. These applicants also had to meet research expectations, express a mature Christian faith, and be able to sign our doctrinal statement. These factors narrowed the field considerably even before I conducted the first round of interviews. However, it still took significant time for my colleagues and me to develop a short list of candidates who seemed to be a "best fit" for our department. As in all searches, we would look at a candidate's past experience to predict his or her future performance with us.

If I were on the committee to choose a leader for the early church, I can guarantee you the Apostle Paul would never make my short list. Based on his past performance, he wouldn't come close. Can you picture the accomplishments listed on his résumé? They would include: guarded coats at the stoning of Stephen (Acts 7:58), approved the execution of this first Christian martyr (Acts 8:1), dragged male and female believers out of their homes in Jerusalem to put them in prison (Acts 8:3), and traveled to Damascus to extradite Christian men and women from the area and take them back with him for trial (Acts 9:1–2). This prior experience was not only a mismatch with the required skill set, it was the antithesis of what the early Christian church needed in its leadership. This would be the same as if my faculty search short lists had included an atheist who dedicated his or her life to destroying all forms of elementary, secondary and higher education institutions. Choosing Paul for leadership made no sense by human standards. Everyone was understandably taken aback by Paul's reputation, including those whom Jesus had specifically called to teach him and work with him.

Luke references Paul, first known as Saul, in the book of Acts, mentioning him prior to his conversion to highlight how dangerous he was to the emergent church. Paul's other characteristics are listed in his Letter to the Philippians, where he looks back on his life and states that he was a Hebrew who had been faultless in his legalistic righteousness (Phil 3:4–6). Paul continues in this letter by stating that he counted these and all other credentials as rubbish in comparison to the treasure he had in knowing Christ as his Savior and Lord.

As a Pharisee, Paul was well educated by Gamaliel (Acts 22:3), the leader of the Sanhedrin who had insisted all his students learn Greek poetry in addition to studying the Scriptures. We also know that Paul was a Roman citizen (Acts 22:28) and a tentmaker by trade (Acts 18:3). From these insights, we know that Paul was highly educated in the Scriptures and had privileges and background knowledge that extended his influence in Greek society and the Roman world. His credentials and entrepreneurial skill set connected him to diverse groups and relieved him of total dependency on the young church for his support. The characteristics of Paul listed here are far from exhaustive. Numerous books have been written on the subject of the Apostle Paul that describe him in far greater detail than I have mentioned here. The descriptors listed above, however, are sufficient for our purpose in understanding Paul's life prior to conversion and why Jesus chose him to help guide the young church at such a crucial point in history.

One might wonder why Paul would be included in a book about Jesus' students. Wasn't he more Ananias and Barnabas' pupil than Jesus'? Didn't they mentor him far more extensively than Christ? One could certainly make a case for this stance, except for the fact that Jesus directly taught Paul the most important lesson he would ever learn. After Paul had dedicated his life to eradicating what he thought was heresy by eliminating those he felt had mistakenly believed Jesus to be the Messiah, he learned in a dramatic lesson on a Damascus road that they indeed spoke the truth—the greatest truth he would ever know. Everything he believed about Jesus was turned upside down in one brief conversation that involved just two questions and a revelation: "Saul, Saul, why do you persecute me?" To this, Paul asked, "Who are you, Lord?" Imagine his shock upon hearing, "I am Jesus whom you are persecuting" (Acts 9:4–5).

Only Paul directly saw the Messenger from the heavens, but his fellow travelers witnessed the supernatural event and its effect on Paul. He was not hallucinating from the heat of the journey.

After this miraculous encounter, Paul's traveling companions led him by the hand into the city, where he remained for three days without sight, food, or drink. Paul's personal revelation from Jesus was the start of a transformation that would ultimately lead to the evangelism of the Gentiles and authorship of nearly half of the books in the New Testament, including those that provide the foundation of our Christian theology. Because of this brief encounter on the route to Damascus, Paul contributed significantly to the spread and understanding of Christianity that continues to this day.

## What do we know about Jesus from this interaction?

The Lord personally confronted Paul, speaking directly to him and literally blinding him with the truth on his journey to Damascus. Jesus also communicated to him through visions when he returned to Jerusalem (Acts 22: 17–21, 23:11) and again in Corinth (Acts 18:9–10). It was rare for Jesus to appear to a follower after the time of his earthly ministry, but calling Paul to an enormous task and getting him to change his core convictions entirely would require proof that Jesus was indeed the Messiah. Hearing the voice of Christ himself brought Paul to his knees as he realized how wrong he had been about the Galilean.

Not only did Jesus teach Paul that he was the true Messiah by directly communicating with him, he also communicated with Paul's first mentor, Ananias, through a vision (Acts 9:9–19). I am sure Jesus chose this method because Ananias would have found the message impossible to believe if it came in any other form. We read that Jesus told Ananias to go to a specific address in the city where he would find a man named Saul from Tarsus, who would be praying. Ananias was told that when he arrived there, his first task was to restore Saul's sight.

Upon hearing this directive, Ananias questioned whether he had heard Jesus correctly and whether Jesus really knew who Saul was. In other words, Ananias was saying, "Are we talking about the same guy—the one who puts people like me to death for following you? Is this the person you want me to give back his sight? Considering all the damage he has done to your cause, the least we could do is keep him from visually identifying us. We are all terrified of him."

Astonishingly, Jesus had not made a mistake. He assured Ananias that Saul was indeed the person he wanted him to find to help the church. He even gave Ananias the description of the job he was calling Saul to complete: to evangelize the Gentiles, their rulers, and other Jews.

What would have happened if Ananias had been too afraid to do what Jesus asked him to do? Restoring a person's sight aside, the challenge of meeting with this dangerous individual would be overwhelming to any teacher. Human nature compelled Ananias to list all the reasons for not going to Saul, but his close relationship to Christ compelled him to obey anyway. He went to this previously defiant student and did exactly as Jesus had instructed him to do, restoring his sight, baptizing him, and offering him food. Paul then remained with followers of Jesus in Damascus and began preaching that Jesus was indeed the Son of God in synagogues there. As one could imagine, his listeners were astonished at this change in Paul's beliefs and mission. Since Paul's former Jewish colleagues viewed this change as heretical, they now sought to kill *him*. Paul, the former hunter of Christ-followers, had become the hunted. The Damascus believers helped Paul escape his pursuers by lowering him in a basket through an opening in the city wall.

This event brought Paul to Jerusalem, where he initially found the apostles and elders similarly reluctant to accept his genuine conversion, much less trust him. Had it not been for Barnabas, who advocated for Paul to the fearful group of leaders, Paul might have been permanently excluded from the church. Barnabas conveyed Paul's experience on the Damascus road and testified to his effective preaching of the gospel in synagogues there. As a result, the disciples invited Paul into their community and protected him from those in the city who sought to kill him.

Barnabas later partnered with Paul on a significant missionary journey to the Gentile world. Their relationship continued until

Barnabas advocated again for another individual with a blemished reputation to become part of their evangelizing team. This time, Barnabas wanted John Mark to accompany him and Paul as they returned to the towns where they had preached during their first trip. But Paul objected to this plan because John Mark had previously deserted them. Ever the encourager, Barnabas wanted to give John Mark another chance, but Paul refused. As a result of this disagreement, their missionary partnership ended. From that point on, Paul and Barnabas traveled separately, with each of them choosing a new companion: Barnabas evangelized with John Mark, and Paul partnered with Silas.

It appeared as if Jesus called the least likely person to expand his church. Or did he? Hindsight always offers a useful perspective in seeing how plans worked out well, and I believe this is the case here. Even though Paul would not have made my short list, I can see why, in God's sovereignty, he was chosen for this role. Paul had been specifically prepared for it through his prior experience and education. Jesus called Paul to a task that would require a keen, well-schooled mind, so his education from Gamaliel, which had included Greek culture as well as the Scriptures, was essential. His background as a Pharisee required him to develop expertise in the specific, though unattainable, requirements of the Law. Paul was a Roman citizen, which gave him rights and protections throughout the region that others in the church would not have had. Being unmarried, he could focus exclusively on his mission of bringing the gospel to the Gentiles. All these abilities and circumstances gave Paul credibility with the diverse populations of his ministry. Looking back, he was an outstanding choice for this work, despite all the misgivings the early church and I would have had with his appointment. Jesus was a wise teacher to see Paul's potential and enable him to actualize the mission he had called Paul to accomplish.

## What can we learn from Paul?

I believe there are two lessons we learn from Paul. The first is that transformation is possible. It was particularly important for the early church to see the power of God enacted in Paul's life. While we have many accounts in Scripture of individuals whose lives were mired in sin, such as the prostitute in Simon's home, no other convert was as determined to defeat the early church as was Saul. His prior life was committed to eradicating all teachings and followers of Jesus. His transformation truly exemplified what it meant to repent as Dallas Willard defines it: "to change the way you've been thinking and acting."[1] In *The Divine Conspiracy,* Willard further defines Christ's call for repentance:

> This is a call for us to reconsider how we have been approaching our life, in light of the fact that we now, in the presence of Jesus, have the option of living within the surrounding movements of God's eternal purposes, of taking our life into his life.[2]

No one answered this call more substantively than the Apostle Paul. He states in his First Letter to the Corinthians, "For I am the least of the apostles and do not even deserve to be called an apostle, because I persecuted the church of God. But by the grace of God I am what I am, and his grace to me was not without effect" (1 Cor 15:9–10).

The second lesson we gain is that Paul did not disqualify himself from serving Christ because of his past sins—even when those past sins were significant. Imagine Paul's regret at realizing the harm he had done and the energy he had wasted in committing his life to rooting out an indestructible force. He could easily have taken himself out of the running by simply seeing himself as unworthy of his calling, but his clear understanding of the gospel helped him understand that none of us has earned a position in the kingdom. Our worth comes from God alone. His forgiveness is complete; he wipes our slate clean. Our gratitude for redemption is the basis for our service. In Rom 3:12, Paul writes, "All have turned away, they have together become worthless; there is no one who does good, not even one." Paul understood that no one earns their

---

1. Willard, "Your Place in this World," 2.
2. Ibid., *Divine Conspiracy*, 16.

standing with God; no one deserves forgiveness, but all who ask for it receive it.

Paul could have also disqualified himself if he perceived that his service would create too much of a disruption in the church at this critical point of its development. Initially, this was indeed the case. The apostles feared him, and his former colleagues, the Pharisees, wanted to eliminate him, which placed both Paul and other followers of Christ in danger. His views on behavioral practices for Gentile believers were controversial to many Jewish Christians (Acts 15:1-21). Paul was not an easy fit for this role despite his credentials and influence. Past sins aside, he did not step into a leadership role easily. In many ways, it would have been logical and practical for Paul to have refused the role.

However, having met Christ personally, Paul could no more think of refusing Jesus' call than he could refuse his next breath. He states in Phil 1:21, "For to me, to live is Christ and to die is gain." His sole focus in life was to serve the One who had forgiven him by preaching the truth to a world that did not know Christ.

## What can we learn from Jesus in this interaction?

The conversion of Paul is one of the strongest pieces of evidence that our past does not matter to Jesus; only our present and future are important to him. This teaching of Jesus was puzzling and defeating news for the rich young ruler, for Simon the Pharisee, and for Nicodemus. The privilege of birth and the study of Old Testament law did not count as criteria for entry into God's kingdom. Performing good works of charity and leading a moral life in obedience to this law also did not count. Self-righteous acts could not erase the need for forgiveness from sin. For those who had gained status in their community from having lived an exemplary life of obedience and contributing many good works, this was a grim truth to accept because it destroyed their mistaken assurance of eternal life. After all their efforts, they were in the same position as everyone else—in need of a Redeemer.

However, it was incredibly freeing for those who believed that their past disqualified them from any hope of heaven. Jesus preached the truth that whoever you had been and whatever you had done, you were not disqualified from having a relationship with God and gaining eternal life with him. Although this was incredibly good news to the prostitute who washed Jesus' feet with her tears and dried them with her hair, the individual who most clearly illustrates this truth is the thief who was crucified with Jesus on Calvary (Luke 23:39–42). Because this one criminal recognized Christ's divine identity and ability to forgive his sins, Jesus gave his word that the repentant criminal could enter paradise. Without any opportunity to live righteously after being forgiven, the thief was promised an eternity with God because of his confession.

Unlike the thief on the cross, Jesus did not save Paul at the end of his life. He had work for him to do. He saw great potential for the kingdom in this man from Tarsus, and therefore Jesus did not let Paul's past exclude him from the future Christ envisioned for him. He had given Paul all the prerequisites for his ministry, and, most importantly, he had enabled Paul to see that they were merely tools for his mission and not prideful achievements in and of themselves.

While Jesus confronted Paul directly with the truth of his identity, he also instructed Paul through two mentors, Ananias and Barnabas. Although initially afraid to interact with Paul, they obeyed Christ's call to teach him and advocate for him. I have wondered how Paul's life and the early church's influence might have been different if either Ananias or Barnabas had not trusted Christ enough to engage with Paul—if they had instead sided with reason and refused to meet with him or advocate for him to their fellow believers. The outcome might have changed if Ananias and Barnabas had let their fears overwhelm them, but they both answered Christ's call even before they saw Paul's potential for bringing the good news of salvation to the Gentiles. Ananias pushed logic aside and stepped out in faith to meet Paul's physical needs and answer his theological questions. Similarly, Barnabas's continuous support and encouragement not only enhanced Paul's role in spreading the gospel message, it enhanced John Mark's contribution as well.

## What can we, as educators, learn from this interaction?

As teachers, we will be challenged by those students whose academic or behavioral reputations initially cause us to dread having them in class or at least question whether they are worth our time or investment. We know before meeting them that we will be required to make an inordinate effort to reach these students and enable them to learn. However, these are the very students who most need a teacher who does not give up on them—a teacher who, like Barnabas, accepts them and encourages them to succeed. They need a teacher who models Christ to them as Ananias did for Paul.

To be an effective encourager, a teacher must first believe that students truly can improve and grow. Carol Dweck writes of this in her discussion of fixed and growth mind-sets and their relationship to learning.[3] If you believe that intelligence and personality are generally fixed, then you believe change is really not possible. Success just verifies your intelligence, but failure causes you to question whether you are, in fact, smart. However, if you believe in a growth mind-set, you see intelligence and personality as malleable. Change is possible through effort. Failure is viewed as just one stepping-stone on the way to learning new skills or concepts.

We might all generally agree with the growth mind-set mentality. Yet don't we all know someone who says, "I'm no good at art" or "I just can't do math"? Perhaps we even think this about ourselves. Dweck's work has served as a catalyst for improving instruction in several subject areas that had formerly been perceived as "talent-dependent," such as mathematics,[4] a curricular area that has long been burdened with stereotypes about who can or cannot be successful in mastering it.

---

3. Dweck, *Mindset*, 4–14.
4. See Boaler, *Mathematical Mindsets*.

Unfortunately, teachers may question the ability of some students to improve and may even communicate this belief in subtle and overt ways. During my doctoral studies, I interviewed an undergraduate who was intent on becoming an elementary third grade teacher. I will never forget his response to my follow-up question, "Why third grade?" He replied, "Because my third grade teacher said I would never amount to anything, and I want to be sure that no third grader in my classroom will ever hear that message."

Amazingly, this young man took a potentially defeating prediction and became empowered by it. Not only did he seek to disprove his teacher's negative expectation, he sought to correct the professional wrong she had committed for future generations of students. This is rare. The level of expectation we communicate to students, either through our words or nonverbal behaviors, often becomes a self-fulfilling prophecy. As this example illustrates, educators hold a great deal of power that could potentially harm students for a long period of time.

Fortunately, teachers can also have a significantly positive impact on a student, as illustrated by the late Christian educator Howard Hendricks, who had a difficult childhood that resulted in tumultuous early elementary school experiences. After being told by his fifth grade teacher that he would most likely end up in prison,[5] he encountered a very different type of teacher in sixth grade. Miss Noe met him at the door on the first day of class with the words "Oh, you're Howard Hendricks. I've heard a lot about you." However, she went on to say, "But I don't believe a word of it!"[6]

Hendricks got a fresh start from this teacher and went on to graduate from college, complete graduate studies, serve as a pastor, become a seminary professor, and serve for eight years as chaplain to the Dallas Cowboys. This legacy turned out quite differently than his fifth grade teacher's prediction. Hendricks largely credits his sixth grade teacher as the catalyst for his academic transformation.

    5. Hendricks, *Teaching to Change Lives*, 28.
    6. Delgado, "Fruits of His Labors," 1.

Although Paul's spiritual transformation occurred immediately, educational transformation in a student most often requires a great deal of any teacher's time and patience. With this type of student, we often see patterns of "two steps forward, one step back." There will be many days when we question whether our commitment and coaching are having any effect at all and whether this type of student can ever break away from his or her past habits. Yet from Jesus' interaction with Paul, we see how important it is to base our rapport with all students on their future rather than their history.

It is critical that we hear from students who perceive their schooling as a negative experience in order to create space for establishing a more positive relationship. Raider-Roth's research suggests a paradigm of four arenas: helping students locate and develop their voice; listening to their voices; creating regular practices that are responsive to students' expressed ideas, concerns, and work; and finally, creating an environment that supports teachers in getting to know their students well.[7] Through this model, we communicate to these students that they matter to us as individuals and not just as learners.

While we need to remain committed to these individuals, we must also realize that a student's progress in academic, social, and emotional development may require more than we, as classroom teachers, can offer them. Equally important to "being there" is determining when a troubled student's challenges require a specialist's expertise. This may involve our advocating for professional counseling, making a referral for special education services, or notifying a social worker or child welfare services to investigate family issues. Like Ananias, we can work to ensure that a student's physical needs are met. Like Barnabas, we can advocate on behalf of our student to provide a safe environment and appropriate learning conditions that will enable him or her to thrive. Yet we must also recognize when there is a need for additional professional help. However, especially when others must be brought in to assist the child or adolescent, it is vitally important that we work

---

7. Raider-Roth, *Trusting What You Know*, 152–53.

to maintain our connection with the student so we don't imply that we see him or her as no longer being our responsibility.

Since we, like Howard Hendrick's sixth grade teacher, Miss Noe, may be the first educator to connect with these students through hope rather than judgment, it will likely take considerable time to develop the mutual trust necessary for a sustained positive relationship. We will need to endure occasions when these students test the limits of our commitment to them as we continue faithfully in correcting their missteps and applauding their approximations. We will need to remind them of our belief in them and their ability to turn things around. Like Jesus' relationship with Paul, we will need to communicate how much they matter to us. To teach like a disciple, we can never give up on our most challenging students.

12

# Parting Words

AS WE REFLECT BACK on these ten interactions, we can conclude that Jesus' classroom contained a group of extremely diverse learners. In Mary Magdalene, we find a heartbroken student. In the rich young ruler, we find a student who craved success. In the woman who touched Jesus' cloak in the crowd, we find a student who needed complete healing from a traumatic past, and in Jairus, we find a parent desperate for help. In the Samaritan woman, we find a student who needed acceptance.

In the early days of the Apostle Peter's education, we see a student who craved attention. In the well-educated and intellectually capable Nicodemus, we find a student who needed to be challenged. In the Apostle John, we see a similarly gifted but quiet student. Through Simon, we find a judgmental student whose cultural and religious prejudice prevented him from seeing anything of value in an individual who was very different from himself. At the other end of the spectrum, we find Mary and Martha, students we would want to please even when it would require us to compromise our goals. And finally, in the early days after the Apostle Paul's conversion, we find a student everyone wanted to avoid.

These individuals comprised quite a heterogeneous class for the Master who taught them over 2,000 years ago. And yet their issues are still the subject of a great deal of current educational research. Through his interactions with these students, Jesus addressed poverty, cultural and religious differences, socio-economic class, the effects of trauma, attention-seeking behavior, identity issues, emotional crises, prejudice, and oppositional behavior. The descriptive portraits of these students from Scripture mirror the lives of our students today far more accurately than any Winslow Homer or Norman Rockwell painting from the nineteenth or twentieth century.

Yet Jesus is regarded as a remarkable teacher not because he recognized and addressed these complex issues but because he recognized and related to the individuals who faced them. He saw these students first as complete human beings before he looked to their struggles or advantages. In truly seeing them, he moved beyond their deficiencies; he recognized their strengths. He saw the courage and keen mind of the woman at the well in Sychar. While he saw hospitality in Simon notwithstanding Simon's judgmental nature, he also saw love and respect from a woman previously entrenched in prostitution as she expressed heartfelt gratitude for her redemption. He saw the loyalty and resilience of Mary Magdalene. He saw the devotion of John and the genuine transformation of Paul. He saw resilient trust in Mary and Martha despite their great disappointment when he did not give them what they had initially requested. He saw boldness in Peter's impulsive nature. He saw Nicodemus' strong desire to know truth. He saw sincere faith and determination in a woman who brushed against him in a crowd.

Seeing these individuals and their needs, the Master Teacher communicated truth and love through a highly individualized approach. He offered his compassion and presence to Mary Magdalene, yet he was demanding and uncompromising to the rich young ruler despite, or rather because of, his love for this man. To the woman at the well he offered acceptance as well as respect for her spiritual knowledge, yet for Nicodemus, Jesus challenged the Pharisee's knowledge and rejected his way of thinking about spiritual matters. For Peter, Jesus was patient yet persistently corrected the disciple each time he became self-focused. For the prostitute, Christ offered reassurance, but for Simon, her accuser, Christ posed provocative questions in order for this student to change his perspective of others. For the woman in the crowd, he offered healing and reconciliation with both her community and his Father. For the two grieving sisters, he offered hope and then enabled them to see the results of that hope. To John, he offered his accessibility and love, while for Paul, his approach could best be described as "tough love." In all these situations, Jesus offered his knowledge—they all learned something vitally important from him—as well as his regard for his students. The characteristics of his instruction were ones we can all aspire to model.

Teacher preparation comprises three broad categories: knowledge, skills, and dispositions. The knowledge component encompasses the spectrum of students' development and how they learn best at each stage. It also includes an understanding of the historical and current issues in education that have prevented or continue to prevent all students from reaching their learning potential. Finally, it involves the content to be taught, or the curriculum, as well as the professional standards that structure the content to be learned at each grade level. In essence, the knowledge component encompasses *what* you teach.

Skills involve the full range of professional practices, or the observable aspect of teaching. They include the various instructional approaches or methods you use to enable your students to learn the content, keeping in mind their developmental stages as well as their interests and experience levels. This component includes implementing research-based strategies for helping students with particular backgrounds or profiles learn effectively. In essence, the skills component is *how* you teach.

The third component is dispositions, or the attitudes, values, and core beliefs you hold about teaching. Are you patient, understanding, and encouraging of all students? Are you responsible, persevering, and resilient in meeting your many roles as an educator? Do you work hard to make your content accessible to all learners, and do you work to make yourself available to your students? In this way, it includes both personal and professional character traits. To summarize, the dispositions component is the *manner in which* you teach.

All three components are essential for effective teaching and learning. Although you cannot be an effective educator without strong content knowledge or pedagogy that is appropriate for both your discipline and your students' age levels, dispositions are what usually make or break teacher-student relationships. While not easily assessed, your attitudes about teaching and learning affect every aspect of your professional practice. How you consistently relate to students, colleagues, administrators, and parents is reflective of your dispositions or character.

Jesus is a wonderful model of all three components. Because of his divine nature, he knew everything, but in each interaction he also knew what specific lesson his student needed to learn. He clearly understood his content as well as the developmental needs and experiential background of his learners.

Since each approach was individualized, we see that Jesus drew upon a remarkable skill set in knowing when to listen and when to speak up, when to challenge and when to affirm. But he did more than speak the truth in a way that was accessible to his diverse students; he spoke the truth in love. While his truth was consistent across all his student-teacher interactions, Jesus' love for each learner guided his unique approach. His was the perfect balance of truth and love in instruction. Merely speaking the truth would have only served to condemn each student. Just loving each of his students would not have prompted them to change their thinking; they would have continued in their mistaken beliefs and lost the opportunity for redemption and a relationship with God.

We have evidence of Jesus' uncompromising truth in his encounters with both the rich young ruler and Nicodemus. Neither man gave evidence of his decision to change his way of thinking or his actions at the end of Jesus' lesson. Jesus taught them with love but saw the responsibility to *accept* his teaching as theirs alone despite the consequences of a wrong choice. He let both men walk away without giving evidence that they had achieved his objective. As we know from Scripture, God "wants all people to be saved and to come to a knowledge of the truth" (1 Tim 2:4), so their failure to accept the truth he was offering them had to be difficult for the Master Teacher to witness. As educators, we have all experienced this sense of loss when students have failed to understand the importance of what we are teaching, even when there are no eternal consequences at stake.

Jesus gave one final, significant lesson to his apostles right before he ended his earthly ministry. His parting words to them, also known as the Great Commission, became the ultimate homework assignment. In Matt 28:19–20, we read:

> Go and make disciples of all nations, baptizing them in the name of the Father and of the Son and of the Holy Spirit, and teaching them to obey everything I have commanded you. And surely I am with you always, to the very end of the age.

As Christ's followers, the disciples were to carry the good news of redemption to every individual on planet Earth. This was a huge challenge made possible only because he would remain with them. His expectation was extremely high, yet he gave them the tools and mentorship to enable them to complete it. His parting words have been passed on to every generation of disciples, including you and me.

Whether we teach in a public or private school, this assignment is ours to complete. By the manner in which we engage students and their families, we are to reflect the same dispositions Christ modeled in his own teaching. Depending on our context, we may not be able to preach the gospel in words, but as his disciples, our lives should so mirror the ways in which Christ demonstrated his regard for his own students that ours are drawn closer to him. On many days teaching will be overwhelming, but we have his assurance that he will be with us, regardless of our context.

One poignant illustration of faith-influenced instruction is the depiction of the afterschool at Saint Ann's of Morrisania Episcopal Church in Jonathan Kozol's *Ordinary Resurrections*.[1] As an extension of the school day, the women of the African American and Hispanic congregation offered children both academic and spiritual encouragement through the practical means of providing a safe environment, help with homework, a warm meal, and moral

---

1. See Kozol, *Ordinary Resurrections*.

guidance in one of New York's poorest neighborhoods, the Bronx's Mott Haven community. Kozol, an outsider in several aspects, was impressed with the program offered at the church each day after school concluded.

In describing Miss Katrice, one of the women who faithfully served up dinner and spiritual advice to the eighty or so elementary school students attending, Kozol wrote of her reluctance to leave at the end of what had to be a tiring evening for her. "'Jonathan,' Katrice once told me, 'no one runs from good.'"[2] I am sure this observation mirrored the reason so many children and the other adults spent their late afternoons together. The Saint Ann's program was good in both its qualitative and virtuous definitions. Students experienced affection, safety, wisdom, and care through the steadfast service of Christian women like Miss Katrice.

"No one runs from good" is my favorite quotation in the entire book. It serves as a reminder of what we, as Christian educators, should offer our students—a safe yet challenging learning environment, rich content, a skill set, and relationships that are wholesome and nourishing. Like Jesus observed in his own students, the women of Saint Ann's saw the group of children in their care not for their poverty, single-parent homes, or learning struggles, but as individuals who loved to experience fun yet showed compassion to each other when one of their peers faced hardship. As a result of this perspective, the afterschool at Saint Ann's became a true haven for families in their community. Through their efforts, these women transformed the kitchen and hallways of Saint Ann's into a genuine sanctuary of the church, affording peace, grace, and comfort to the students they loved.

I trust that as one who aspires to teach like a disciple, you will continue to put into practice the knowledge, skills, and dispositions you have learned in your own preparation program. But I also hope that as you look out over your group of students, you will see Peter, John, Mary Magdalene, and even Paul among their faces. I pray that you will teach them like a disciple.

2. Ibid., 30.

# Bibliography

Banks, James A., and Cherry A. McGee Banks. *Multicultural Education: Issues and Perspectives*. 7th ed. Hoboken, NJ: Wiley, 2010.

Boaler, Jo. *Mathematical Mindsets: Unleashing Students' Potential through Creative Math, Inspiring Messages and Innovative Teaching*. San Francisco: Jossey-Bass, 2016.

Bonhoeffer, Dietrich. *The Cost of Discipleship*. New York: Simon & Schuster, 1959.

Brooks, Paul. "Teacher Leniency/Strictness and Students' Grades." *Resources in Education* (1990) 1–18. ERIC (ED 322140).

Bruner, Frederick Dale. *The Gospel of John: A Commentary*. Grand Rapids: Eerdmans, 2012.

Cain, Susan. *Quiet: The Power of Introverts in a World That Can't Stop Talking*. New York: Broadway, 2013.

Cleary, Beverly. *Henry and Ribsy*. New York: Morrow, 1954.

Codell, Esmé Raji. *Educating Esmé: Diary of a Teacher's First Year*. Chapel Hill, NC: Algonquin, 2001.

Coerr, Eleanor. *Sadako and the Thousand Paper Cranes*. New York: Puffin, 1977.

Coplan, Robert J., and Kathleen Moritz Rudasill. *Quiet at School: An Educators' Guide to Shy Children*. New York: Teachers College, 2016.

Craig, Susan E. *Trauma-Sensitive Schools: Learning Communities Transforming Children's Lives, K–5*. New York: Teachers College, 2016.

Danielson, Charlotte. *Enhancing Professional Practice: A Framework for Teaching*. 2nd ed. Alexandria, VA: Association for Supervision and Curriculum Development, 2007.

Delgado, Berta. "Fruits of His Labors." *Dallas Theological Seminary: Howard G. Hendricks*. Reprinted from *The Dallas Morning News*, January 4, 2003. http://www.dts.edu/about/profiles/Howard_G_Hendricks.

DeNisco, Alison. "Does Common Core Hurt Introverted Students?" *District Administration*. December 2015. http://www.districtadministration.com/article/does-common-core-hurt-introverted-students.

Dweck, Carol S. *Mindset: The New Psychology of Success*. New York: Ballantine, 2006.

## BIBLIOGRAPHY

Furner, Joseph. M., and Sally Robison. "Using TIMSS to Improve the Undergraduate Preparation of Mathematics Teachers." *Issues in the Undergraduate Mathematics Preparation of School Teachers* 4 (2004) 1–20. ERIC (EJ835515).

Godsey, Michael. "When Schools Overlook Introverts." *The Atlantic*, September 28, 2015. http://www.theatlantic.com/education/archive/2015/09/introverts-at-school-overlook/407467/.

Goldsmith, Martin. *Jesus and His Relationships*. Carlisle, UK: Paternoster, 2000.

Graham, Donovan. *Teaching Redemptively*. Colorado Springs, CO: Purposeful Design, 2003

Green, Chris. "The Fear of Public Speaking." *Chris Green Communication*. 2015. http://http://www.chrisgreencommunication.com/fear-of-public-speaking/.

Gundry, Robert H. *Commentary on the New Testament*. Peabody: Hendrickson, 2010.

Gutek, Gerald L. *Historical and Philosophical Foundations of Education*. 5th ed. Boston: Pearson, 2011.

Haycock, Kati. "Good Teaching Matters . . . A Lot." *Thinking K–16* 3 (1998) 1–14.

Hendricks, Howard. *Teaching to Change Lives: Seven Proven Ways to Make Your Teaching Come Alive*. Colorado Springs, CO: Multnomah, 1987.

Isaacson, Walter. *Einstein: His Life and Universe*. New York: Simon & Schuster, 2007.

Jensen, Eric. *Teaching with Poverty in Mind: What Being Poor Does to Kids' Brains and What Schools Can Do About It*. Alexandria, VA: Association for Supervision and Curriculum Development, 2009.

Kaplan Thaler, Linda, and Koval, Robin. *Grit to Great: How Perseverance, Passion, and Pluck Take You from Ordinary to Extraordinary*. New York: Crown, 2015.

Keller, Timothy. *Generous Justice: How God's Grace Makes Us Just*. New York: Dutton, 2010.

Kierkegaard, Søren. *Works of Love*. New York: Harper Collins, 2009.

Klem, Adena M., and James P. Connell. "Relationships Matter: Linking Teacher Support to Student Engagement and Achievement." *Journal of School Health* 74 (2004) 262–73.

Kounin, Jacob. *Discipline and Group Management in Classrooms*. New York: Holt, Rinehart, & Winston, 1970.

Kozol, Jonathan. *Ordinary Resurrections: Children in the Years of Hope*. New York: Harper Collins, 2000.

Ladson-Billings, Gloria. *The Dreamkeepers: Teachers of African American Children*. 2nd ed. San Francisco: Jossey-Bass, 2009.

———. "Q & A with Gloria Ladson-Billings." *Learning Connections* (Fall–Winter 2013). https://news.education.wisc.edu/news-publications/learning-connections/archive/2013-fall-winter/q-a-with-gloria-ladson-billings.

# BIBLIOGRAPHY

Layne, Steven L. *Igniting a Passion for Reading: Successful Strategies for Building Lifetime Readers.* Portland, ME: Stenhouse, 2009.

Lederhouse, Jillian N. "Personal Faith and Professional Practice." *Educational Horizons* 90 (2011–2012) 13–15. ERIC (EJ955118).

———. "You Will Be Safe Here." *Educational Leadership* 56 (1998) 51–54. ERIC (EJ570154).

Lewis, C. S. *Mere Christianity.* New York: Harper Collins, 1952.

———. *Narnia, Cambridge and Joy 1950–1963.* Vol. 3 of *The Collected Letters of C. S. Lewis*, edited by Walter Hooper. New York: Harper Collins, 2007.

———. *Surprised by Joy: The Shape of My Early Life.* Orlando, FL: Harcourt, 1955.

Lowry, Lois. *Number the Stars.* New York: Houghton Mifflin, 1989.

Marzano, Robert J., Jana S. Marzano, and Debra J. Pickering. *Classroom Management That Works: Research-based Strategies for Every Teacher.* Alexandria, VA: Association for Supervision and Curriculum Development, 2003.

Maxwell, Lesli A. "U.S. School Enrollment Hits Majority-Minority Milestone." *Education Week*, August 19, 2014. http://www.edweek.org/ew/articles/201 4/08/20/01demographics.h34.html.

National Governors Association Center for Best Practices and Council of Chief State School Officers. *Common Core State Standards.* Washington, DC: National Governors Association Center for Best Practices, 2010.

NGSS Lead States. *Next Generation Science Standards: For States, by States.* Washington, DC: National Academies, 2013.

Nieto, Sonia. "Public Schools and the Work of Teachers." In *Why We Teach Now*, edited by Sonia Nieto, 9–20. New York: Teachers College, 2015.

Noddings, Nel. *Caring: A Relational Approach to Ethics and Moral Education.* 2nd ed. Berkeley: University of California Press, 2013.

———. *Critical Lessons: What Our Schools Should Teach.* New York: Cambridge University Press, 2006.

Palmer, Parker. *The Courage to Teach: Exploring the Inner Landscape of a Teacher's Life.* San Francisco: Jossey-Bass, 1998.

———. *To Know as We Are Known: Education as a Spiritual Journey.* San Francisco: Jossey-Bass, 1993.

Orlev, Uri. *The Island on Bird Street.* New York: Houghton Mifflin, 1984.

Raider-Roth, Miriam B. *Trusting What You Know: The High Stakes of Classroom Relationships.* San Francisco: Jossey-Bass, 2005.

Richter, Sandra L. *The Epic of Eden: A Christian Entry into the Old Testament.* Downers Grove, IL: InterVarsity, 2008.

Schmidt, William. "Seizing the Moment for Mathematics." *Education Week*, July 18, 2012. http://www.edweek.org/ew/articles/2012/07/18/36schmidt.h31.html.

Schwartz, James E. "Christians Teaching in the Public Schools: What Are Some Options?" *Christian Scholar's Review* 26 (1997) 293–305.

# Bibliography

Seligman, M. E. P. *Learned Optimism: How to Change Your Mind and Your Life.* New York: Knopf, 2006.

Steele, Dorothy M., and Cohn-Vargas, Becki. *Identity Safe Classrooms: Places to Belong and Learn.* Thousand Oaks, CA: Corwin, 2013.

Stevens, Heidi. "We All Benefit as Schools Get More Diverse." *Chicago Tribune*, September 8, 2015.

Stitt-Gohdes, Wanda L. "Student Teachers and Their Students: Do Their Instructional and Learning Preferences Match?" *Business Education Forum* 57 (2003) 22–27. ERIC (EJ664042).

Stross, Randall E. *The Wizard of Menlo Park: How Thomas Alva Edison Invented the Modern World.* New York: Crown, 2007.

Sullivan, Peter, and Pat Lilburn. *Good Questions for Math Teaching: Why Ask Them and What to Ask (Grades K–6).* Sausalito, CA: Math Solutions, 2005.

Von Brummelen, Harro. *Walking with God in the Classroom.* 3rd ed. Colorado Springs, CO: Purposeful Design, 2009.

Wenham, G. J., et al., eds. *New Bible Commentary: Twenty-first Century Edition.* Downers Grove, IL: Intervarsity, 1994.

White, E. B. *Charlotte's Web.* New York: Harper Collins, 1952.

Wiggins, Grant, and Jay McTighe. *Understanding by Design.* 2nd ed. Alexandria, VA: Association for Supervision and Curriculum Development, 2005.

Willard, Dallas. *The Divine Conspiracy: Rediscovering Our Hidden Life in God.* San Francisco: Harper Collins, 1998.

———. "Your Place in This World." Commencement address at Greenville College, Greenville, IL, May 2004. Transcribed and edited by Steve Bond for the Holman Christian Standard Graduate's Bible, 2005. http://www.dwillard.org/articles/artview.asp?artID=109.

Winebrenner, Susan. *Teaching Gifted Kids in the Regular Classroom.* Minneapolis, MN: Free Spirit, 2001.

Wolterstorff, Nicholas. *Educating for Life: Reflections on Christian Teaching and Learning.* Edited by Gloria Goris Stronks and Clarence W. Joldersma. Grand Rapids: Baker, 2002.

Witherington, Ben, III. *The Gospel of Mark: A Socio-Rhetorical Commentary.* Grand Rapids: Eerdmans, 2001.

Wright, S. Paul, Sandra P. Horn, and William A. Sanders. "Teacher and Classroom Context Effects on Student Achievement: Implications for Teacher Evaluation." *Journal of Personnel Evaluation in Education* 11 (1997) 57–67.

Made in the USA
Las Vegas, NV
06 September 2023